The Year of the Poet XI

December 2024

The Poetry Posse

inner child press, ltd.
'building bridges of cultural understanding'

The Poetry Posse 2024

Gail Weston Shazor
Shareef Abdur Rasheed
Teresa E. Gallion
hülya n. yılmaz
Noreen Snyder
Tzemin Ition Tsai
Elizabeth Esguerra Castillo
Jackie Davis Allen
Mutawaf Shaheed
Caroline 'Ceri' Nazareno
Ashok K. Bhargava
Alicja Maria Kuberska
Swapna Behera
Albert 'Infinite' Carrasco
Michelle Joan Barulich
Eliza Segiet
William S. Peters, Sr.

~ * ~

In order to maintain each poet's authentic voice, this volume has not undergone the scrutiny of editing. Please take time to indulge each contributor for their own creativity and aspirations to convey their uniqueness.

hülya n. yılmaz, Ph.D.
Director of Editing ~
Inner Child Press International

General Information

The Year of the Poet XI
December 2024 Edition

The Poetry Posse

1st Edition : 2024

This Publishing is protected under Copyright Law as a "Collection". All rights for all submissions are retained by the Individual Author and or Artist. No part of this Publishing may be Reproduced, Transferred in any manner without the prior **WRITTEN CONSENT** of the "Material Owners" or its Representative Inner Child Press. Any such violation infringes upon the Creative and Intellectual Property of the Owner pursuant to International and Federal Copyright Laws. Any queries pertaining to this "Collection" should be addressed to Publisher of Record.

Publisher Information
1st Edition : Inner Child Press
intouch@innerchildpress.com
www.innerchildpress.com

Copyright © 2024 : The Poetry Posse

ISBN-13 : 978-1-961498-49-5 (inner child press, ltd.)

$ 12.99

WHAT WOULD
LIFE
BE WITHOUT
A LITTLE
POETRY?

Dedication

This Book is dedicated to

Humanity, Peace & Poetry

the Power of the Pen

can effectuate change!

&

The Poetry Posse

past, present & future,

our Patrons and Readers &

the Spirit of our Everlasting Muse

*In the darkness of my life
I heard the music
I danced...
and the Light appeared
and I dance*

Janet P. Caldwell

Table of Contents

Foreword .... *ix*

Preface .... *xiii*

Renowned Poets .... *xv*

    Imru' al-Qais

The Poetry Posse

Gail Weston Shazor	1
Alicja Maria Kuberska	11
Jackie Davis Allen	17
Tzemin Ition Tsai	25
Shareef Abdur – Rasheed	33
Noreen Snyder	39
Elizabeth Esguerra Castillo	45
Mutawaf Shaheed	53
hülya n. yılmaz	63
Teresa E. Gallion	69
Ashok K. Bhargava	75
Caroline Nazareno-Gabis	81

Table of Contents ... *continued*

Swapna Behera	87
Albert Carassco	95
Michelle Joan Barulich	101
Eliza Segiet	109
William S. Peters, Sr.	117

December's Featured Poets — 125

Kapardeli Eftichia	127
Irena Jovanović	135
Sudipta Mishra	143
Til Kumari Sharma	149

Inner Child Press News — 157

Other Anthological Works — 201

Foreword

Renowned Poets

Imru' al-Qais

A Pre-Islamic Poet

I chose this poet because I have traveled to the area he was born, where he was raised and probably where he was inspired as a young man. He was born in pre- Islamic Arabia. He is considered the father of Arabic Poetry. He was born in 501 A D died in turkey 544 A D. He didn't live a long time by today's standards. He was able to establish himself as an important influence during and after his life time, in the field of poetic expression. During the Islamic period he was acknowledge as a major figure in the world of poetry. The Arabs were known for the great memories and it was through poetry, many historical events were preserved and remembered. He was the author of one of the seven odes in the famed collection of pre -Islamic poetry, The AL MU'allaqat was a style he was credited with inventing. There many poets who in the Islamic era who became reciters of the Holy Quran and memorizers of the sayings of the Prophet Muhammed (PBUH). For many decades a poem was selected to be located on the corner of the

Kaa'bah. Im-ru lived in Constantinople Moved to Ankara, where he fell ill and died in 544. He was on his way back from seeking the Roman emperor's help in taking back his father's kingdom.

Mutawaf Shaheed

Now Available

www.innerchildpress.com/world-healing-world-peace-poetry

Coming Soon

www.innerchildpress.com/the-anthology-market.php

Preface

We, **Inner Child Press International, The Year of the Poet** and **The Poetry Posse** welcome you.

WOW . . . a decade +. We continue to be excited as now finishing our 11th year of Production for **The Year of the Poet**.

This particular year we have chosen to feature renowned poets of history. We do hope you enjoy. Read ~ Learn.

For those of you who are not familiar with our story, back in 2013, a few of us poets got together with the simple intention of producing a book a month. That was our challenge. Since that time the enterprise has blossomed and brought forth a fruit that seems to keep on growing as evidenced as we enter 2023.

Our purpose is simple. Through our lyrical words and verse, we not only wish to share our poetic works, but we also have the poetic naiveté to believe that we can assist in the growth of consciousness of the things that have an effect our collective humanity. Therefore, we welcome your readership. For more about what we are attempting to accomplish, have a look at our Publishing Web Site . . . www.innerchildpress.com. If you would like to know a bit more about this particular endeavor please stop by for a visit at :

www.innerchildpress.com/the-year-of-the-poet

Over the years, Inner Child Press has been socially active to bring awareness and catalog through literature the things that have an impact upon our world and its inhabitants. We have solicited, produced, underwritten and published quite a few volumes to that end. For more insight you may wish to visit : www.innerchildpress.com/the-anthology-market. If you are a writer, poet, or activist, you would be advised to keep a eye out for upcoming volumes should you desire to participate. All readers are welcomed as well. Note, that there is a myriad of published volumes that are available as a FREE PDF download as well as available for purchase at affordable prices.

We at this time extend to you our well wishes for your own personal journey and hope that you consider including us as a travel companion.

Bless Up

Bill

William S. Peters, Sr.

Publisher
Inner Child Press International
www.innerchildpress.com

Renowned Poets
Imru'al-Qais Junduh bin Hujr al-Kindi

(501 AD-544 AD)

December 2024

by hülya n. yılmaz, Ph.D.

Imru'al-Qais Junduh bin Hujr al-Kindi is generally considered to be the father of Arabic poetry. He has been acknowledged by the Prophet Muhammad, by ʿAlī, the fourth caliph, and by Arab critics of the ancient Basra school as the most distinguished poet of pre-Islamic times. By some literary critics, the origin of the Arabic ode has also been attributed to this poet. His famed *Al-Muʿallaqāt* is a collection of his seven odes originating from the pre-Islamic, i.e., the Jahiliyya period of Arabs.

The first six stanzas of *Al-Muʿallaqāt* find Imru'al-Qais in deep melancholy as he stands before his beloved's former home. The lovesick poet honors her memory while he stresses the impermanent human condition:

Let's stop and cry over the memory of a lover and a place, in the drop of the valley between Dakhul and Haumal

And Taudih and Mikrat. Their traces haven't been wiped out from what wove them back and forth between the southern and northern winds.

Look at antelope droppings on its alleys, its tracks like seeds of pepper

As if it's only been a morning since the day they departed, and I'm at a nearby thorn tree, splitting desert gourds,

And standing near it are my companions on their travel animals, saying, 'Don't suffer from sorrow, remain firm.'

But my healing is a matter of spilling tears. So, is there a trace here from a reliable artist?

At this point, I will dare a quantum leap from AD to our times in order to build a "reliable" (line 13) bridge between the Bedouin poet of our focus in this month of December 2024 and us, The Poetry Posse and the featured poets. For I view the status of each of our contributors as that of an "artist" (line 13).

◇ ◇ ◇ ◇

Selected Sources:

Encyclopedia Britannica
The Hanging Poem of Imru' al-Qays
The Poems of Imru' al-Qais

◇ ◇ ◇ ◇

hülya n. yılmaz, Ph.D.

Professor Emerita, Liberal Arts
(Penn State, U.S.A.)
Director of Editing Services,
Inner Child Press International (U.S.A.)

*Poets . . .
sowing seeds in the
Conscious Garden of Life,
that those who have yet to come
may enjoy the Flowers.*

Poets, Writers . . . know that we are the enchanting magicians that nourishes the seeds of dreams and thoughts . . . it is our words that entice the hearts and minds of others to believe there is something grand about the possibilities that life has to offer and our words tease it forth into action . . . for you are the Poet, the Writer to whom the Gift of Words has been entrusted . . .

~ wsp

Poetry succeeds where instruction fails.

~ wsp

Now Available

www.innerchildpress.com/the-anthology-market.com

Gail Weston Shazor

Gail Weston Shazor

Gail Weston Shazor is a lover of words. She is fond of the arcane, unusual and the not yet words.

Coining words at an early age, there was often a bit of trouble with teachers, but she always had her mother and aunt to back up her choices in expression. Born in Mississippi, she spent her early years with her grandparents. Each of the four left very careful influences on her pre-schooling. She learned in turn how women worked in and out of the home and how men worked in and out of the home to support the family. She learned that a lack of proper schooling was not the only way to learn and understanding life was a great teacher. As in most rural families of color, women had a greater chance of formal learning. Both of Gail's grandmothers read out loud to the family whether it was the bible or the newspapers and important documents to their spouses.

Gail Weston Shazor has authored (so far) Notes from the Blue Roof, A Overstanding of an Imperfect Love, HeartSongs and Lies My Grandfather's Told Me. The number of anthologies is too many to list with the premier accomplishment of one of the contributors to The Year of The Poet. Gail will always lend her ink to community projects and will purchase the books of fellow poets in the Inner Child Press family.

YWHW

i say YWHW from You
i breathe Your very name into my mouth
And the whisper covers the air i taste
You name yourself everlasting
Alpha and Omega
Am that you Am and
It is sufficient for my limitedness
And i breathe after You-Abah
In the midst of my day
In the middle of my life
i find that You are here
In the same place i find myself
It is not that You have ever left
i moved
And now that i have returned
i say yes
And draw close to You
For in this i am refined after my rescue
Storms rarely run in a straight line
And i have been buffeted around
And i have run headfirst into the wind
Even though You told me no
i could not hear for the listening
To my flesh senses
So my doxology has become this
i am greatfilled to the inked
And to the said
And to the whispered breath of You
i say yes to the wind across my face
The salty sea on my lips that flavors
My independence of dependence
For You are my choice

This one of abundant living in the midst
Of practicing to yield to You
i am your child of water
i am your adult of giving
i accept who You made me to be
So i live You in my waking
And in every love of my life
i expand, reach and fill much farther
Than i can ever hope to do alone
And though i am not perfect
You
Are

standing in the wilderness shouting

I am here, arms wide open
Waiting on my creator to
Speak
Talk
Move
Give
Me something for you
So that I can be obedient
To fall on my knees in fasting
Eating only the words of
Life
Death
Birth
Stillness
With all the power of first
And all the waiting of last
Beginning and end
The words of the crafter
Poet
Writer
Lyricist
Deliverer
And I will ink it quick
Placing it everywhere you are
So that you can see and hear

What is in store for you
Me
They
Us
All
There is never a time

When the word was not offered
Only when it was not received
And not called forth to teach
Truth
Wisdom
Correction
Love
For that is our purpose
And why were made
And what we have been
Ordered to spread among
Ghettos
Cities
Fields
Hearts
Til all has been healed I remain
Jusbill in the Wilderness

wake up

You knead my soul
Until my bones ache
I hear your cries in my sleep
And yet
I cannot find you in the morning
In the full awakening of daylight
For that is when you are muted
When you can be seen
Unaided by policies and laws
And it is too hot to be awake
Too cold to move around
Too arid and windy to wander about
Too weak to move against the tide
In the before
You hung around ghetto corners
Waiting on programs
Stood at the end of long rows
Waiting on conscription
Sat in the back of the room
Waiting to be aborted
And covered in coal dust
Yet they say they are here for you
A shell game of benefits
Have you looking for the misdirection
Because you know it's there

You have seen it
And have felt it
And have tasted it
Like bile in the back of a dry throat
I hear your cries
In my sleep

On the edges of darkness into daylight
I want to soothe you
Rub your back and circle
Your belly with the span of my heart
I will bring you clean water to drink
If you don't hide from me
When I am consciously aware
That you do not enjoy
The freedoms that I do
The love that I do
The dissension and confusion that I do
Because you do not live
In the comfort and safety of knowing
That some things are only dreams
And my heartache will ease
My bones will heal and my belly will
Be filled
If not today, then tomorrow
But you
Will always long for us to
Wake
Up

Gail Weston Shazor

Alicja Maria Kuberska

Alicja Maria Kuberska

Alicja Maria Kuberska – awarded Polish poetess, novelist, journalist, editor.

She is a member of the Polish Writers Associations in Warsaw, Poland and IWA Bogdani, Albania. She is also a member of directors' board of Soflay Literature Foundation, Our Poetry Archive (India) and Cultural Ambassador for Poland (Inner Child Press, USA)

Her poems have been published in numerous anthologies and magazines in : Poland, Czech Republic, Slovakia, Hungary,Ukraina, Belgium, Bulgaria, Albania, Spain, the UK, Italy, the USA, Canada, the UK, Argentina, Chile, Peru, Israel, Turkey, India, Uzbekistan, South Korea, Taiwan, China, Australia, South Africa, Zambia, Nigeria

She received two medals - the Nosside UNESCO Competition in Italy (2015) and European Academy of Science Arts and Letters in France (2017). Ahe also received a reward of international literary competition in Italy „ Tra le parole e 'elfinito" (2018). She was announced a poet of the 2017 year by Soflay Literature Foundation (2018).She also received : Bolesław Prus Prize Poland (2019), Culture Animator Poland (2019) and first prize Premio Internazionale di Poesia Poseidonia- Paestrum Italy (2019).

Imru al-Qays
Arab Prince

The stars shine with a cool glow over the desert.
Between grains of sand, longing slips through.
The wind tirelessly erases traces of past time
and mournfully sings a song of parting with a beloved.
In the silence, verses of love and desire are born.
Memory replays the happy moments of lovers.
Memories take on a bitter taste
like the ripe fruit of colocynth.
Centuries have passed,
yet the zephyr still whispers love spells.
It inscribed the poem on the stone at the Kaaba,
so letters of gold would capture
the beauty of the desert and feelings.

Lecce

The city of stone lace
resembles a bride
dressed in a baroque gown –
seemingly modest, yet rich.
Whorls and flourishes adorn
the snow-white fabric.
The young girl walks among
the sculpted garlands of altars.
Into a wreath of oak leaves
she adds the Latin word *leccio*.
Here comes Venus, born of foam –
the patroness of artists and lovers.
She needs no golden adornments
to shine in the temple's dim light.

Autumn in Belgrade

The city sprawls between
two shades of blue.
It seeks solace, silence
in the arms of the Danube and Sava.
Against the clear sky,
the orthodox churches domes gleam.
Into the rustling of lush plane trees
are weaved the solemn songs.
Time does not hurry
to take away the city's Art Nouveau charm.
The wind arranges arabesques from leaves,
the sun gilds balconies and roofs.

Tsar Alexander I gazes
from the portrait in the hotel lobby.
He was here yesterday and will be tomorrow
– he will not abandon the white city.
See you in the future.
The autumn wind will lead me here.
I am like threads of spider silk
drifting on the wave of events.

Jackie Davis Allen

Jackie Davis Allen

Jackie Davis Allen, otherwise known as Jacqueline D. Allen or Jackie Allen, grew up in the Cumberland Mountains of Appalachia. As the next eldest daughter of a coal miner father and a stay at home mother, she was the first in her family to attend and graduate from college. Her siblings, in their own right, are accomplished, though she is the only one, to date, that has discovered the gift of writing.

Graduating from Radford University, with a Bachelor's of Science degree in Early Education, she taught in both public and private schools. For over a decade she taught private art classes to children both in her home and at a local Art and Framing Shop where she also sold her original soft sculptured Victorian dolls and original christening gowns.

She resides in northern Virginia with her husband, taking much needed get-aways to their mountain home near the Blue Ridge Mountains, a place that evokes memories of days spent growing up in the Appalachian Mountains.

A lover of hats, she has worn many. Following marriage to her college sweetheart, and as wife, mother, grandmother, teacher, tutor, artist, writer, poet and crafter, she is a lover of art and antiques, surrounding herself, always, with books, seeking to learn more.

In 2015 she authored *Looking for Rainbows, Poetry, Prose and Art*, and in 2017, *Dark Side of the Moon*. Both books of mostly narrative poetry were published by Inner Child Press and were edited by hulya n. yilmaz in 2019, *No Illusions. Through the Looking Glass*, which was nominated to be considered for a Pulitzer Prize by the publisher and editor of Inner Child Press, ltd.

http://www.innerchildpress.com/jackie-davis-allen.php
jackiedavisallen.com

Who Was He?

He was a young man, in his prime.
Most likely, handsome! He was a prince-of-a-guy!
Wealthy, and yes, he had a roving eye!

A bad boy, living for the moment, in search
Of the pleasurable, the forbidden, enjoying the good life.

A playboy, no stranger to the scandalous, he was a smooth operator,
With a penchant for the ladies-of the night.

"Self-indulgent" to an excessive degree, his actions,
his reputation, heaped flames of shame upon his father's head.

Hungry, always, ever, thirsty, he sampled temptation.
Yielding to its attraction, a striking figure with generous gift of gab,
He could be found night or day, beneath the influence of the vine.

You wouldn't be surprised to discover, that from an early age, that young man began penning poems, perhaps some rhymes.
A singer of song, he may have had a melodic, lilting voice.

Tragedy, like a dark cloud, descended, and as fate intervened,
He, his life, his conscience, and his attitude changed.

Motivation came, to exact revenge, in retribution, a way to seek retribution for his father's death, his father, the King!
To exact revenge, he had to act. And so, he did.

You might be forgiven for thinking him a modern-day performer, actor, composer. But no, he was the son of a King!

Inspiration for this poem came from reading Wikipedia, about the prince Imru' al-Qais.

As Thorns in Achilles Heel

Didacticism, how wide the prevalence,
The essayists, handmaidens, imparting bias,
Propaganda tainted without truth, rhetoric,
Painted with Stalinist prose, nothing else.

Their dreams, fruitless, impotent by negligent intent
Overtly dependent upon riding backs, by those
Whose dreams are devoid of a fiscal conscious,
Robbing Peter to pay Paul: a fatal design.

Ignorant of the fact, or from avarice, greed,
That which one sows is that which one reaps.
Chanting, whining, liberally, literally, their
Knuckles worn bare, in pockets not their own.

An insidious cloying fever, heads bowed before
Fame of the drawing card, a cult of those
For whom personal responsibility belongs only,
Solely...(they chant)...to the other side.

Has common sense withered and died, that a
Nation of sheep are led in race over the cliff,
By one, in disguise, each one coveting, jealous,
Wanting, claiming that to which he has no right?

George Orwell and 1984 have come and gone, yet
The vision, about a body left unchecked, remains.
The Wolf still lives, wields control, pronouncements
Are as infected thorns in a nation's achilles heel.

Self Portrait

From all of the colors, which ones will you
Use to paint your likeness, your self portrait~
The colors of kindness, of loyalty,
The colors of forgiveness, of great love,
Or, will you paint in self indulgent shades?

From which of your most pronounced attributes
Will character evolve as true likeness?
Will your pose be dark or cheery, a face
Transparent or concealed behind deceit?
Does it matter which colors will be used?

Within the framework of your humanity,
There exists traits, both the good and the bad,
Some highlighted by notoriety
Some hidden, like secrets in a diary,
Waiting, praying that they've been forgiven.

A book by its cover, we should not judge.
Yet, why then do you, with your self portrait
Discard some images as unworthy?
Are you ashamed to face mirror's disgrace,
Deny the extent of your vanity?

You peruse the contents of books, so too,
The illustrations and ask yourself,
Is there a price to pay in the painting
Of a self-portrait? And, if there is, what price need
Anyone to pay to paint each and every day?

Tzemin Ition Tsai

Tzemin Ition Tsai

Dr. Tzemin Ition Tsai comes from the Republic of China(Taiwan). In addition to being a professor of literature at a university, he is more committed to writing poems, novels, and proses. He is also an editor of "Reading, Writing and Teaching" academic text, an International editor of "Contemporary dialogues" literary periodical in Macedonia, and Vice-Chairman of the International Jury of the SAHITTO INTERNATIONAL AWARD in Bangladesh, and a columnist for "Chinese Language Monthly" in Taiwan.

In a wide range of literary creations, he is particularly fond of interesting stories or novels, and writing articles or poems about the feelings of nature and human beings. He has won many national literary awards. His literary works have been anthologized and published in books, journals, and newspapers in more than 55 countries and have been translated into more than 24 languages.

Remembrance of Chang'an

Upon halting my steed upon the broken bridge,
The wind bears scents afar, Qinhuai's shadow gleams serene.
It floats so lightly, as if thy graceful sleeves do dance.
The willows of Chang'an, where we once walked, laughing as petals fell,
Now remain but a desolate terrace, bathed in cold moonlight, recounting partings and tangled fates.
The gentle rain enshrouds, yet temple bells pierced the shroud,
Softly drawing the echo of the whispered tones.
Before the sacred lamps, I did a beseech, yearning they form restored to light.

Amidst the shadowed mountains, countless deities rest in their azure calm.
The pine winds murmur, might they carry dreams where we meet anew?
Would I not offer a thousand cups of pure tea, in tribute to time long departed?
Time flows onward, beside the River Luo, I hear songs crest waves, catching lines of fishermen's lore.
The lotus sways, weaving itself into yesterday's dust.
Might the clouds, perchance, know?
Thy light-footed steps—
Hast thou borne thy soul to join their ethereal shapes?
And the waters—have they ferried my lingering dreams to thee?

The night's lamp dims, at last, the candle's tears fall,
Yet undying is that which—
Is etched into the very marrow of longing.

Chang'an's walls, lofty still upon my backward glance,
But all else, the people, their stories, are gone.
The lone crane wails: the fractured clouds seek their retreat.
Should we meet again amidst the rivers and mountains,
Let strings of the zither weave our words,
And moonlight vow to heaven and earth: our hearts bound, unbroken.

Lofty Aspirations Across Millennia

From humble lands I rose,
With blade and steed, clad in chaos-stirring green.
Under the Han banner, I swept binding foes of the northern plain,
Sword's edge gleaming bright across nine realms.
Against tempest waves, I struck.
Time flows, its autumns fleeting beneath the mist of borderlands.
Through the swirling paths of Shu, clouds ascend,
Lances fall, tents scatter, resounding cries echo deep.

With golden arms and iron steeds, who dares not kneel?
On Taishan's peak I stand,
Singing boundless tunes, defying saddle-bound invaders.
No bowing brow, no servitude to fleeting power.
Let trials sharpen my blade, deeds carve mountains asunder.
This life seeks but one—an enduring name in the annals of time.
Heroic spirits, fleeting as dreams,
Leave vows etched upon swords and scrolls,
As the Yangtze roars eternally through the ages.

Lonely Journey in the Yellow Sands

The morning wind sweeps past,
The Yellow River churns, its waves coiled like dragons.
Endless desert stretches forth,
Camel caravans take on the shadowy form of the Great Wall.
Countless footprints of the past are scattered by the wind,
In the fleeting moment of time,
Ancient legends are lost upon this silent, desolate land.

In the vast desert, a solitary plume of smoke rises straight,
As the setting sun turns the earth a golden hue.
Like the carving of time's blade,
Light and shadow intertwine to paint a vast, empty scroll.
The traveler journeys a thousand miles,
Only the stars guide him north and south.
Each star, like a lantern in the eyes of an old friend, faint, yet eternal.

Beyond the frontier, snow presses down on the poplar trees like silver robes,
Each snowflake that falls carries with it the cold of the past,
The poplars silently stand guard,
Blooming the sharpness of life in their solitude.

In Guanzhong, plum blossoms bloom fiercely, defying the cold winds.
The traveler steps boldly, unafraid of the perilous path,
Each step as though traversing the tunnel of time,
The unwavering strength within,
Crossing thousands of mountains and rivers,
Only to behold the grandeur of the Nine Provinces.
The other shore of the spirit is the source of all dreams and desires.

In the eyes, a thousand leaves and flowers,
The vastness and magnificence of the earth,
Every sunset and sunrise serve as a guide to the journey ahead,
In the boundless desert, he seeks only the invisible faith to lead him onward.

Shareef Abdur Rasheed

Shareef Abdur Rasheed

Shareef Abdur-Rasheed, AKA Zakir Flo was born and raised in Brooklyn, New York. His education includes Brooklyn College, Suffolk County Community College and Makkah, Saudi Arabia. He is a Veteran of the Viet Nam era, where in 1969 he reverted to his now reverently embraced Islamic Faith. He is very active in the Islamic community and beyond with his teachings, activism and his humanity.

Shareef's spiritual expression comes through the persona of "Zakir Flo". Zakir is Arabic for "To remind". Never silent, Shareef Abdur-Rasheed is always dropping science, love, consciousness and signs of the time in rhyme.

Shareef is the Patriarch of the Abdur-Rasheed Family with 9 Children (6 Sons and 3 Daughters) and 41 Grandchildren (24 Boys and 17 Girls).

For more information about Shareef, visit his personal FaceBook Page at :

https://www.facebook.com/shareef.abdurrasheed1
https://zakirflo.wordpress.com

Imru
B 496 AD D 565

son of tribal king
born Arabia
very complicated deep
poet from young age
loved sensual poetry
loved wine
loved many women
king papa didn't
threw him out
eventually king assassinated
by opposing tribe
wine drinking poet,
women chaser became a
warrior seeking to avenge
the death of his father
he conducted a sustained
attack on the Asad tribe
for years
all the while he was considered
the greatest poet in pre-Islam Arabia
he continued to write love poetry
also, tearful remembrance
paying tribute to his fallen comrades
coming from seeking more military
aid from a Caesar
that Caesar got word that Imru
was having an affair with his daughter
he gave him a garment as a gift
laced with a poison that gets into
the body through the skin
it killed him while traveling
on the grave of a women, he laid
dying and said whoever from near
or far who has soil over their body are kin,

wild

what the hell
more madness the
better
so much for majority rule
if majority acting a fool
would you get on a plane
piloted by a madman
who never flew a plane
if the majority of passengers
said take-off, would you?
the population contains
deaf, dumb, blind, bias
tribal zombies
humans void of humanity
seeking the good and plenty
the wrong way
they created their own prison
cell
what the hell locked themself in
self-inflicted cult members already
doing time
in the prison of the mind
majority rules even though
majority fools?
democracy or dem a crazy?

Life in a Nutshell..

welcome to a glimpse of heaven/hell
just a taste of where you may dwell
haste makes waste so contemplate well
before you choose where forever you decide
to reside
remember your fate that awaits from which no one
can hide
nor shuck, nor jive square your life away before you die
you don't know the day before it arrives
then it will be too late to strive
when your fate without warning arrives
so you go ahead and ignore instead, like you got rocks
in your head
so you act like life will last eternal until the angel of death
shows up getting personal
now what ?..........datz watsup!
the day for which we should prepare for and pray
your soul's taken gently and your destination is
the kingdom paradise, good ' n ' plenty, milk ' n ' honey
no more evil world and all its fake monopoly money

Noreen Snyder

Noreen Snyder

Noreen Ann Snyder has been writing since she was a teenager. She writes a variety of different topics. Her favorite poetic forms are Sonnets, Blitz, Haiku, Tanka, and Free Verse. She always learning different poetic forms.

Noreen Ann Snyder is a poet, writer, and an author of five books, (four books are co-authored with her late husband, Garry A. Snyder.) Her poetry is in several Inner Child Press Anthologies. She is the founder of The Poetry Club on Facebook.

Imru' al-Qais

Imru' al-Qais, an Arabian poet,
the wandering king
His dad kicked him out of his court
because of his poetry and his style of living,
and that's how he became the Wandering King.
His poetry reflected his life experiences,
love, loss, nature, and warfare,
the inventor of so many styles, including
the Qasida, the Classical Arabic Ode.
He's the father of the Arabic poetry.
His masterpiece can be found
in Mu'allaqat, (The Hanging Poems.)
His poetry is raw, the kind where
you'll say "Wow,"
one-of-a-kind, talented poet,
the one you won't forget.

Reflect

Reach until you cannot stretch.

Roar loudly like a lion.

Reduce the negativity and

refuse defeat and despair.

Reflect who you are and what you want.

Respect yourself and others.

Rejoice and be glad you're alive.

Be Inspired

Time to mend
not the end
just a beginning
pick up the pen,
and write
like it's your last night.
Write from your heart and soul,
write from your guts deep within.
Just pick up the pen
let the pen guide you,
let the ink drip
forming words.
Be inspired, get inspired!
Don't be afraid!
Be you!
Just write
and write, and speak, and speak.
And remember read and read
to get and to be inspired.

Elizabeth E. Castillo

Elizabeth Esguerra Castillo

Elizabeth Esguerra Castillo is a multi-awarded and an Internationally-Published Contemporary Author/Poet and a Professional Writer / Creative Writer / Feature Writer / Journalist / Travel Writer from the Philippines. She has 2 published books, "Seasons of Emotions" (UK) and "Inner Reflections of the Muse", (USA). Elizabeth is also a co-author to more than 60 international anthologies in the USA, Canada, UK, Romania, India. She is a Contributing Editor of Inner Child Magazine, USA and an Advisory Board Member of Reflection Magazine, an international literary magazine. She is a member of the American Authors Association (AAA) and PEN International.

Web links:

Facebook Fan Page

https://free.facebook.com/ElizabethEsguerraCastillo

Google Plus

https://plus.google.com/u/0/+ElizabethCastillo

In the Shadows of Imru Al-Qais

In the desert's heart, where the sandstorm sighs,
Beneath azure skies, where the lone hawk flies,
Imru Al-Qais traversed, with a soul made of fire,
His heart a wild steed, with a spirit to aspire.

Lost in tales of love, both bitter and sweet,
He penned his longings in verses complete;
Of a maiden so fair, with a gaze like the moon,
In the echoes of night, he'd whisper her tune.

By the gushing springs and the palm trees' shade,
He'd craft his lament, where lovesick dreams played.
With a lyre of stars, and the breeze as his guide,
He'd sing of his passion, with the dunes as his bride.

But the winds would not tell of his joys or his pains,
They carried his verses through mountains and plains,
And the world became witness to heartache's embrace,
As the poet found solace in poetry's grace.

O Imru Al-Qais, in a realm forged by fate,
With the weight of your love, bore a soul desolate,
Yet in every heartbreak, a legacy blooms,
For the echoes of longing find life in tombs.

So let the sand swirl and the stories be spun,
In the tapestry woven, your spirit shall run,
For the heart that knows sorrow, in beauty takes flight,
In the shadows of history, you'll shine ever bright.

Velvet Moon

In the velvet cloak of night,
The Moon hangs high, a silver sight,
A lantern casting gentle beams,
Illuminating whispered dreams.

She sings to tides, a muse of seas,
A guardian of secrets in the breeze,
Her craters tell of ages past,
Of lovers' vows and shadows cast.

In her glow, the world transforms,
Fields shimmer, and the wild norm swarms,
With fireflies dancing in her light,
A ballet woven through the night.

Oh luminous orb, you wax and wane,
A playful lover, a dance of gain,
You guide the lost with your soft embrace,
A tranquil balm, a timeless grace.

Beneath your gaze, the heart confides,
In starlit whispers where hope abides,
You cradle dreams, both big and small,
A witness to the rise and fall.

So here I stand, in reverent awe,
As you cast your gaze, without a flaw,
Oh Moon, my muse, forever bright,
A beacon of wonder in the endless night.

Nature Goddess

In the cradle of the cosmos, where silence softly breathes,
Lives a spirit clad in green and gold, in gentle winds she weaves,
Her laughter ripples through the rivers, her whispers dance with trees,
For in her arms, the earth awakes, beneath her watchful ease.

The morning sun awakes her heart, with a symphony of light,
Awakening the blossoms, painting fields in colors bright.
From mountain peaks to valleys deep, her canvas stretches wide,
With every shade of life she breathes, in her embrace we bide.

She cradles clouds, and stirs the seas, with storms that roar and play,
With tender hands, she nurses life, at night and during the day.
A tapestry of ecosystems, every thread a story told,
Of ancient roots and feathered flight, in her arms, life unfolds.

Yet in her eyes, a glimmer shows, a worry, deep and real,
For as we claim her cherished gifts, our greed becomes the steel.
Oft have we dulled her vibrant hues, defiled her sacred ground,
Forgotten that the pulse of life in harmony is found.

With every tree we choose to fell, with every river run,
We test the limits of her grace, beneath the sinking sun.
But still she offers second chances, with resilience, she

stands tall,
A reminder of our fragile bond, the tether that we call.

So let us heed her whispered calls, in every leaf and stone,
To cherish what is given us, and not to stand alone.
For Mother Nature's heart is vast, her love, a ceaseless tide,
In unity, we find the strength to walk, together, side by side.

Mutawaf Shaheed

Mutawaf Shaheed

C. E. Shy has been writing since the seventh grade. He continued writing through high school, until he became more involved in sports. After his graduation, he worked at the White Motors Company where he wrote for the company's newspaper. He started a column called: "The Poet's Corner." That was his first published work.

www.innerchildpress.com/c-e-shy.php

Dust Storm

Caught up in the storms of dust, bringing sayings with winds at their backs.
Blending in with the mirage sown by the dust. Thoughts blasted by sand
making issues clearer, nearer to being transparent by the poet's magic
hands. Clear night skies. Eyes focused on lights that arrived a billion years
ago. Too far away to grasp their meanings as they twinkle off and on.
Imagination working from hot to cold. From a land that was told by sages
from ages long ago. Fulfilling a destiny written before he wrote a single
curved line in the sand or any other place in the land.

Almost Maybe

I think I can find a little refuge in the ink,
to let my thought's rise and sink as they
will. Looking for comfort on the bottom
line. Trying to seek shelter from some
subhuman beasts. At least for a decade
or more. Unable to understand or define
a life form created from crime.

Sperm packed with germs let loose to
undermine human kind. Almost no clean
water left to drink. Not enough letters to
describe what kind of creature you're
standing next to. your blood is not enough
to fix a freak's need to fulfill their unnatural
needs. Serving time with slime while I try
to find some breathing room.

Still being dazed by the familiar phrases
that justify their very existence. Watching
the mischief makers describe made up
situations, while their soulless bodies are
put on hold until they catch on fire.
Ambitions filled to the brim with filth.
The people mind's lined with laminated
lies, no need for open eyes, if they open
them, then all they'll see is rated X TV.

Misery sells, the media is full of it. Holding
dreams together with scotch's tape, in the
background are flawed landscapes designed
by rape artists. The rights of today are the
left overs of tomorrow. Falling further and

Mutawaf Shaheed

further from the center of attention, when
words of beauty are spoken of, your name is
never mentioned. If I saw you, like you see
yourself, I'd be blind to.

Rated triple AAA in destruction. Scurrying
around the earth mind boggled, disrupting
everyone and everything you see. A tour
guide to genocide and it's practical applications.
the poster boy for horror stories. Nobody counts,
they are just numbers in a perpetual stacked
deck. Voices raised high, asking the reasons
why their babies must die?

You smile and grin saying, let them say it again.
Let them scream on to the top of their lungs.
They can't do a damn thing about it. That's their
conscience, not mine. Next to them standing in
the line is a killer of mine. They have a voice, not
a choice. I can't remember ever telling them that
they did! You, don't think you actually have a seat
at this table? Do yah? Not even almost maybe.

Alleged

It's been alleged that this country is
mine. Where is the deed that I can't
seem to find? Why would I pay taxes
to someone so unkind, if this spot
where I live was really mine? Reaching
for the pencil that will help me erase
the shades of gray.

The ones that don't want to go away.
Some of my ideas may viewed as being
cynical. Knowing that they aren't reckless,
assists me reaching the pinnacle of the
influences of what my words will do.

Can't stay away from the ER because
he won't stop lying. Reality represents
me, if and when the truth is told. It
won't be told by them about me. Being
twisted and bent out of shape are the
new dimensions that align themselves
with the mischief makers.

Sentences constructed sent out like
mis- guided missives. Shopping with
conmen, make what people buy much
easier. Manipulated minds can't seem
to find a straight path to anywhere.

Standing on a square suffering from
round house kicks. She found joy
derived from the pool boy, after being
dug from the bottom of the barrel. He

should have lowered his expectations
and his gaze then been happy with the
minimum wage.

When they got finished, she screamed,
RAPE! Nothing one can say that would
Make it go another way, because being
screwed up and astray is their path to
heaven, by the way of a flawed percept-
ion.

Doing to others what they have done,
means, don't do it to them, just keep
doing it to others. Married to the idea
that they have been divinely guided,
they should never have to suffer.

Human sacrifices strewn all over the
globe. Animals , insets, flowers and
plants don't stand a chance against the
pests among the sub-human branch.

Cutting no deals with cut throats.
Avoiding conversations with back
stabbers. Another day of staying
above the fray, this is the way to
keep my values intact.

No more unlocked doors or walking
down the streets after dark. The parks
close now by the time the sun sets.
That's the time when the miscreants
get lodged and let loose, to become
the things that go bump in the night!

I wish I didn't have to walk with my Glock!
Using words full of deception to acquire
his neighbor's processions. That kind of
logic is completely sick and incoherent.

These are the things that happen when
the brain drains and is left without any
kind of direction. Crimes committed are
then acquitted, depends on who the hell
you are?

In your case, the facts are omitted, so you
can't get with it, or get a chance to even
know who the heck you were or who you
now are.

Mutawaf Shaheed

hülya n. yılmaz

hülya n. yılmaz

Of Turkish descent, hülya n. yılmaz [sic] is Professor Emerita (Penn State, U.S.A.), Director of Editing Services (Inner Child Press International, U.S.A.), and a trilingual literary translator. Before her poetry and prose publications, she authored an extensive research book in German on cross-cultural literary influences.

Her works of literature include a trilingual collection of poems, memoirs in verse, prose poetry, short stories, a bilingual poetry book, and two books of poetry (one, co-authored). Her poetic offerings appeared in numerous anthologies of global endeavors.

hülya writes creatively to attain and nourish a comprehensive awareness for and development of our humanity.

hülya n. yılmaz, a traveler on the journey called "life" . . .

Writing Web Site
https://hulyanyilmaz.com/

Editing Web Site
https://hulyasfreelancing.com

disillusioned

pity to all who like i
think that one could return
to some thing or someone
who was built there before,
who breathed there before

Imru' al-Qais lived through
such a despair times and times again
his beloved, no longer in her old place,
filling her lifeline with an empty space

al-Qais' odes or "hanging poems"
would not suffice to replace
his utterly-felt heartache

pity to all who like i
think that one could return . . .

cemeteries

the blame is on me
each time, i have missed
the burial ceremonies of my loved ones

did i lament their void?
did i cry in their absentia?
did i feel like an inadequate human?

i still do
at each of my breaths

these days, i seek only those stories
where i, as the antagonist, visit cemeteries
to pay my due service to those beloveds of mine
who passed on - sans my dearly loving presence

snow

flakes larger than life

upon the freshly cut grass

nothing permanent

Teresa E. Gallion

Teresa E. Gallion

Teresa E. Gallion was born in Shreveport, Louisiana and moved to Illinois at the age of 15. She completed her undergraduate training at the University of Illinois Chicago and received her master's degree in Psychology from Bowling Green State University in Ohio. She retired from New Mexico state government in 2012.

She moved to New Mexico in 1987. While writing sporadically for many years, in 1998 she started reading her work in the local Albuquerque poetry community. She has been a featured reader at local coffee houses, bookstores, art galleries, museums, libraries, Outpost Performance Space, the Route 66 Festival in 2001 and the State of Oklahoma's Poetry Festival in Cheyenne, Oklahoma in 2004. She occasionally hosts an open mic.

Teresa's work is published in numerous Journals and anthologies. She has two CDs: *On the Wings of the Wind* and *Poems from Chasing Light*. She has published three books: *Walking Sacred Ground, Contemplation in the High Desert* and *Chasing Light*.

Chasing Light was a finalist in the 2013 New Mexico/Arizona Book Awards.

The surreal high desert landscape and her personal spiritual journey influence the writing of this Albuquerque poet. When she is not writing, she is committed to hiking the enchanted landscapes of New Mexico. You may preview her work at

http://bit.ly/1aIVPNq or ***http://bit.ly/13IMLGh***

Response to Imru al-Qais Poem

The stars open their curtains
to expose you in night's light
while you take what is not yours.
After the long night, your love
will beg for mornings kiss to the earth
in the stream of first light.

The dust of weariness cannot hold you back.
The birds in the valley serenade you.
You will not confess today
that you took everything from this woman
and left her in cold, bloody sheets.

Because you could not face the truth.
Love cannot be forced
with violent overtures of power.
In the long run, you lose.
Left to the ages with an empty heart.

Seasonal Massage

Fall teases on approach,
then rushes like a whirlwind
as colors fall to earth.
The soil is flush with fullness.
Hunger is released to the wind.

We cling to the last massage
as fall folds into winter light.
A sudden cold, dampness
brings a wave of gray skies
that lull us into sleep.

There is always reason for hope.
Spring always comes
with a flame of sweetness
to kiss the meadows.
Our nostrils tremble in spring's smell.

High Stakes

You cannot shake off
the anxiety that chases your bones.
That is your sign to work hard.
Change is coming.

Swallowing becomes difficult.
Indigestion sings in your chest.
Transformation is biting at your heels.
That is your sign to move forward.

Open your arms.
Accept your blanket of desire.
The truth wants to lay its head
on the warm blanket you hold.

Look into your third eye.
Spirit is waiting to initiate you.
You must walk alone
into your new realms of joy.

Ashok K. Bhargava

Ashok K. Bhargava

ASHOK BHARGAVA is a poet, writer, inspirational speaker and a literary consultant. He has attended poetry conferences in Italy, Turkey, India and Philippines. His latest book "Riding the Tide" about his battle with cancer has been translated and published in Arabic, Hindi, Telugu and Bengali languages. He is a contributing writer to several anthologies worldwide including World Poetry Almanac 2014. He has been published in numerous print and online magazines.

Ashok has won many accolades including Poet Ambassador to Japan, Kalidasa International award, World Poetry Lifetime Achievement award, Writers Beyond Borders Peace award and Tapsilog Leadership award for his community involvement. He is founder of Writers International Network Canada Society to discover, nourish, recognize and celebrate writers, poets and artists and to assist them to network with the community at large. He is the author of eight books of poetry and one anthology. He is Artist-in-Residence at Moberly Arts & Cultural Centre and also co-edits the literary section of The Link Newspaper.

The Lost King
For Imru' al-Qais

Waves of restless sand dunes
rock tribal loyalty
avenging slayers of the king.

For the slain father
he renounced his passions -
poetry, wine, women and
fought to extract
revenge in blood.

He spent the rest of his life
to regain what was lost..

I imagined asking what he missed most.
He answered, pointing to the fingers writing poems.

He didn't miss scandalous orgies or wine
but poetry that
his father didn't want him to write.

Let it Go

Life is always shifting, forming.
Nothing lasts forever, let go of fears.
Alone at night, I sing to myself -
What looks real isn't real, let go of it.

Let me tell you I'm living a life
that was about to leave me
quietly   without   fanfare   hugs or kisses.

I'll not let it go without celebrations,
giggles and laughter.

We are all made up of broken
and mended hearts.

So we must thank God
for all the joys and blessings.

We are so lucky
to have food to eat
home to live
family to love
and friends.
Could the garden of Eden
be any better?

I'm a Tree

holding the soil
like deeply held
eco-secrets
in my heart.

I sing with winds
I whisper with rivers
I fly with my leaves
I dance with clouds
I'm a tree.

Love me
hug me
don't dismember my limbs
I am your friend
I'm a tree.

Caroline 'Ceri Naz' Nazareno Gabis

Caroline 'Ceri' Nazareno-Gabis

Caroline 'Ceri Naz' Nazareno-Gabis, author of Velvet Passions of Calibrated Quarks, World Poetry Canada International Director to Philippines is a multi-awarded poet, editor, journalist, educator, peace and women's advocate. She believes that learning other's language and culture is a doorway to wisdom.

Among her poetic belts include **Gabrielle Galloni Memorial Panorama International Youth Award** 2022, Panorama Youth Literary Awards 2020, 7th Prize Winner in the 19th, 20th and 21st Italian Award of Literary Festival; Writers International Network-Canada ''Amazing Poet 2015'', The Frang Bardhi Literary Prize 2014 (Albania), Poet Journalist Award 2014 (Tuzla, Istanbul, Turkey) and World Poetry Empowered Poet 2013 (Vancouver, Canada). She's a featured member of Association of Women's Rights and Development (AWID), The Poetry Posse, Galaktika Poetike, Asia Pacific Writers and Translators (APWT), Axlepino and Anacbanua. Her poetry and children's stories have been featured in different anthologies and magazines worldwide.

Links to her works:

http://panitikan.ph/2018/03/30/caroline-nazareno-gabis/

https://apwriters.org/author/ceri_naz/

http://www.aveviajera.org/nacionesunidasdelasletras/id1181.html

Wanderer's Whisper

(Tribute to Imru' al-Qais)
Imru'l al-Qais, The King of Wanderers,
He was born into royalty,
His name echoed in the desert,
The Tales of Thrones soared,
His words are as sharp as warrior's blades,
But his heart adorns his home of love,
The starlit canopy worn grips of fierce,
His soul roamed like people's song,
The rebel poet's unspoken desires
Were written in the stars.
His verses paint the crowns of humanity,
His legacy is a timeless channel of poetry.

Omoiyari

Sometimes the world of words fall short,

Silence speaks volumes,

The spaces between us were misunderstood,

Like unbound footsteps

And raging paces,

If you don't mean the words uttered,

Your feet stomped one's despaired road,

It breathes like a bridging soul,

Rushing care lingers

and empathy shapes   our world,

the gesture finds a gentle spirit,

a call beyond ourselves,

to embrace

all.

(omoiyari- is Japanese concept that means empathy, compassion and deep consideration for others)

Pathways to Excellence

Here's the journey we take,
Stride to find the best of luck,
The era of Enlightenment flashes doors
Of opportunities, of possibilities,
We cross the miles and find the ship,
That sails the ocean of breakthroughs,
Finding innovative solutions and learning,
Like great minds move mountains,
Open gates that trailblaze the myriad schemes,
Where synergies of triumph are resounding bliss,
We stand strong, we walk along.

Swapna Behera

Swapna Behera

Swapna Behera is a trilingual poet, translator, environmentalist, editor from India and author of seven books of different genres including one on children's literature on Environment. She is the recipient of International UGADI AWARD 2019, honoured from Gujurat Sahitya Akademi 2022, 2021 International Poesis Award of Honor as Jury, Pentasi B World Fellow Poet, Honoured Poet of India from Seychelles Government and International awards from Algeria, Morocco, Kajhakhstan, modern Arabic Literary Renaissance of Egypt, International Arts Council Argentina etc. Her stories, poems, articles are published in many International and National magazines and ezines. Her poem A NIGHT IN THE REFUGEE CAMP is translated into 67 languages. She has received over 60 National and International Awards. At present she is the Cultural Ambassador for India and South Asia of Inner Child and the life member of Odisha Environmental Society

Email
swapna.behera@gmail.com

Web Site
http://swapnabehera.in/

Imru al -Qais: the father of Arabic poetry

Imru al- Qais Junduh bin Hujr al- Kindi
the pre Islamic poet from Arab
born at Najd in the late sixth century
the last king of the kingdom of Kindah
passionate about love
author of the Muallaqat (hanging ones)
suspended odes in the framed collection
expelled twice from his father's kingdom for his erotic poetry
he invented the techniques of qasida
his themes were on love, loss, longing, desert landscape
Arab chivalry, seduction of women,
victory of battles, skills with swords and arrows
each line is the combination of two verses
each called a BAYT
a melancholic poet he was
whose poems written on golden letters on the scrolls of linen
hung on the walls of the Kaabba in Mecca
symbolic they are with vivid description
indeed, he is a classical poet and father of Arabic poetry

When a transwoman speaks ....

"On the subject of sex, silence became the rule"

FOUCAULT

I am a sleeping beauty
my beauty trapped inside the cage of my soul
with the body of a man
I need a red gown and lipsticks
I may not have breasts of a woman
I wish to be a mother
What an agony I face for my gender dysphoria and discrimination
I am not a beggar or sex worker
Why should I be segregated?
Why can't I reveal my gender identity?
I am a good dancer, a public speaker
need to express my grief, my potentialities to work
for our culture, humanity and sustainability of nature
Just give me an opportunity
I can teach, reach beyond all boundaries
Here I dedicate my life to all the humanity
Don't ever irritate me or humiliate
I am a queen who has overcome the transit period
 Now I celebrate the peace zone after my surgery
Hold my hand dear community
We will walk together
discuss with me of any political, sociological issues
I too have my views, my rights
as a part of the cosmic entity as you all are
don't throw stones at them
never ever try to make them the sex workers
they are intellectuals
recognise their existence

after my death, I know the police will write my gender identity

Yes, I am a transwoman who glorifies creation
I too stayed in my mother's womb for nine months
crossed the painful journey with
memoirs of experiencing loss of acceptance
discovered myself reconciling my past and present
my vulnerable gender fluidity
transitioning is a journey and not the destination
"help me to grow" is my appeal
empathy or sympathy both I don't need
I just wish to live in my own way
with my ear rings and of course with my voice
that I am a trans woman
a beautiful creation
 I am your friend forever

Oneirataxia

I flow
 to meet my destination
carrying the dead saliva of ash,
resurrected dead body on the pyre
I am a river by the way

I stand
as a pillar
my voice truncated
green monologues surrender
clouds drizzle
 the vision is clear
Save the flora and fauna
I am a mountain by the way

Swapna Behera

Albert 'Infinite' Carrasco

Albert 'Infinite' Carassco

Albert "Infinite The Poet" Carrasco is an urban poet, mentor and public speaker.

Albert believes his experience of growing up in poverty, dealing with drugs and witnessing murder over and over were lessons learnt, in order to gain knowledge to teach. Albert's harsh reality and honesty is a powerfully packed punch delivered through rhyme. Infinite grew up in the east part of the Bronx and still resides there, so he knows many young men will follow the same dark path he followed looking for change. The life of crime should never be an option to being poor but it is, very often.

Infinite poetry @lulu.com

Alcarrasco2 on YouTube

Infinite the poet on reverbnation

Infinite Poetry

www.lulu.com/us/en/shop/al-infinite-carrasco/infinite-poetry/paperback/product-21040240.html

www.innerchildpress.com/albert-carrasco

Imru Al-Qais

What looks like waves of water made of crystal like powder mixed in sand is usually the back drop of my land.
Standing here I sigh of content as I stare at the sky because it's heaven sent.
I was a prince that turned into a poet of kings, in exile I understood why a caged bird sings. When no one was around, "I" was found, "I" is my emotions put into sound.
He gave the naked truth, his verse was bare, he was raw beyond compare, the only thing covered was his body with cloth to protect his skin from the sun and sand from his hair. He braved the monsoon of dunes.
In darkness he brought light, when he spoke his poems were bright, verses of love and war took flight, he had a way with words, his similes and metaphors were tight.
I loved and I've lost, but I've gained from the experience, to me it's still a win because we learn from loss, it's like a second chance to begin what we began in the land of Arabian deserts and wavy sand.
The world knew my voice and my story, in Arabia I'm considered the father of poetry.

Caught in the mix

I was caught up in the mix, ya know poverty, the drive to end poverty, cocaine and heroin,

The streets was the blender that spun with the earth's rotation, the end process was bars, burials and addiction in the pursuit of financial freedom. Unfortunately, my story is the same story for many men, there's not a lot of parents that gave birth in New York in the late 60's and 70's that still have those children due to the mayhem that started in the 80's under Reagan.

It feels like a dream but I know it's true when I look at my bullet wounds and all the funeral cards of my crew and affiliates that were also mixed into that deadly brew. When I rewind time in my head, I see visions that should be beautiful but are mostly ugly because most of the images I see are me surrounded by faces of the dead. I'm at that point in life where if I haven't seen a person in a long time and I see a mutual friend I won't ask "hey how's so and so? because I already know how that convo will end, that way I can picture them blessed with no stress and I'll be able to keep the thought of "I'll see them again". The run to reign caused a lot of pain due to life sentences and those dreaded three days of rain.

Masked up

I made sure to load clips with gloves so no prints stay, when the gats up I'm masked up, no prints on the casings of slugs, no face of the blaz'n thug, that's what you call a clean get away.

After made moves pipes were dismantled to put new pins/hammers and barrels to change strike marks and to remove lands and grooves, nothing was garbage, everything was recycled for more carnage. In broad day while pushn hard yay I taught recruits how to shoot, we sent boxes of ammo to the sky over the 20 and the boot, then it was cans and bottles before they was ready for urban battles, had to get their aim right in preparation for gun fights to possess that evil root. I made marksmen, when the timing was right they'll take one shot that'll take out two men… precise precision. They know how to cover their tracks before they leave like dope fiends with long sleeves, I taught em all of that from experiences in trap. It was a kill or be killed time, you had to be ready to die or in order to live on the C and D grind. While you plot on what moves to make next theirs opps plotting your death, I keep on point watching my surroundings, while you're scheming, I'm already red dotting, holding my breath.

Michelle Joan Barulich

Michelle Joan Barulich

Michelle Joan Barulich was born in Honolulu, Hawaii on the island of Oahu. She started writing poetry and songs with her younger brother Paul. They have written many songs in their teen years. She is currently studying Alternative Medicine and would like to become a Homeopathic Doctor. Michelle loves all kinds of animals and birds; she does wild rehabilitation. She has also rescued rock pigeons that make great pets.

https://www.facebook.com/michelle.barulich

Let Us Stop and Weep

Imru an Arabian poet

Known as the Father of Arabic poetry

As a child he began composing poetry

Like many figures of the early Arabia, they relied on stories

One of his famous quotes was today for drink tomorrow for serious matters

It has been said that after the passing of Imru

The Greeks made a statue of him

To remember his poetry

and his literary and national inspiration.

God's People

I can see myself looking through the mirrored glass
I can feel the pain with every breath
Somebody says your life is down the street
I turn around and I see
Everything makes sense
Now it connects with our spirit
I can feel God's hand touching mine
Through times, I have my highs, and I get my share of lows
I wonder if I'll ever make it
Wishing I could follow in the saint's footsteps
St. Jude, I pray to you
You are the forgotten one
And I had to say all my goodbye's
So, I know you understand
St. Anthony, you are the finder of lost things
Help me find the good in everyone
Help me find God
St. Anthony, there are many times I think of you
St. Mary The Mother of God Your eyes are full of love
Teach me what it means
Thanks for pulling me through
And I dedicate the rosary to you
Jesus,
You are the best example of a man
You are everything to everybody
Guide me to be a part of you Jesus,
I look up to you and with my burning heart
I think of you, And I pray, dedicate, and love you all God's people.

In The Midst of the Night

I hear an angel call
A calling for everyone
There's no more time to waste
And there will never be
No more crying from a child's eye
In the midst of the night
We will be free
In the midst of the night
We will see
A man I knew
Had to prepare to fight
He wrote me a poem
Not more than two lines
For he said he couldn't go on
He said, if we both make it
We will be together
In the midst of the night
We will be free
In the midst of the night
All the children too
Before the night will fall
We will have to fight
We will walk through hell
Before we see the light
before we see
Theres a war going on
Its hate against hate
We will just have to wait
Oh, please come quickly
I hear an angel call
It's for everyone to hear and see
Now the stars are falling

And the fog is rolling out
I can see everyone
Everyone is coming home
In the midst of the night
It will be our sign
The children reunite
In the midst of the night
We will be free
In the midst of the night
Everyone will see
In the midst of the night
We shall be freed.

Eliza Segiet

Eliza Segiet graduated with a Master's Degree in Philosophy at Jagiellonian University.

Received *Global Literature Guardian Award* – from Motivational Strips, World Nations Writers Union and Union Hispanomundial De Escritores (UHE) 2018.

Nominated for the Pushcart Prize 2019, 2021.

Laureate *Naji Naaman Literary Prize 2020*,

International Award Paragon of Hope (2020),

World Award 2020 *Cesar Vallejo* for Literary Excellence. Laureate of the Special Jury *Sahitto International Award* 2021, World Award *Premiul Fănuș Neagu* 2021.

Finalist *Golden Aster Book* World Literary Prize 2020, *Mili Dueli* 2022, Voci nel deserto 2022.

At the international Festival of Poetry CAMPIONATO MONDIALE DI POESIA (2021/2022) she won the title of vice-champion of the world.

Award BHARAT RATNA RABINDRANATH TAGORE INTERNATIONAL AWARD (2022).

Award - *World Poets Association* (2023).

Laureate Between words and infinity *"International Literary Award (2023).*

Revenge
In memory of Imru' al-Qais*

How is it possible that because of his poetry
he was forced to leave the kingdom?
The king had forbidden his son to write....
'It's not appropriate.'

The son
had not yielded to his father's will.
The punishment for his disobedience
was exile.

He began to live
by his own rules.
Gambling, hunting, drinking
and women became his bread and butter.

The awakening came
when
the news of his father's death reached him.
Still one more day after his passing
he continued to play but his reason
was already telling him:
Today is for a drink, and tomorrow for serious matters.**
The latter were to mean revenge for killing his father!

He declared: *Wine and women will now be forbidden to me
until I have killed a hundred Banu Asads (...).*
And he kept his word.

Despite being in exile,
he'd decided to avenge the king's death.
Perhaps he had realized

that all his father wanted was his son's good
though ignoring the fact
that everyone has the right to make their own decisions.
The son had chosen to write.
His poetry transported him
 – through the world, through the centuries, to non-oblivion.

Imru' al-Qais Junduh bin Hujr al-Kindi was an Arab king and poet who lived in the sixth century. He is considered the father of Arabic poetry.
** "Today for a drink, tomorrow for serious business" is one of his most famous quotes.

Translated by Dorota Stępińska

Grief

Old age
may never chance,
it has a chance
to come around.

In the times
when the pace of life
is getting faster
youth can be
overworked
instead of outlived.
It slips away,
leaving insufficiency
and grief.

So many,
very many
lost moments.

Translated by Artur Komoter

Karma

Molded not in the image of others:
– not worse,
– not more foolish,

– or maybe smarter?

These are the ones
who choose the path
to the beauty in the garden of life.

Not those
who know
where the good is, and
where the evil is

but those
who feed with good

will gain the furthest.

Translated by Artur Komoter

William S. Peters Sr.

William S. Peters, Sr.

Bill's writing career spans a period of well over 50 years. Being first Published in 1972, Bill has since went on to Author in excess of 50+ additional Volumes of Poetry, Short Stories, etc., expressing his thoughts on matters of the Heart, Spirit, Consciousness and Humanity. His primary focus is that of Love, Peace and Understanding!

Bill says . . .

I have always likened Life to that of a Garden. So, for me, Life is simply about the Seeds we Sow and Nourish. All things we "Think and Do", will "Be" Cause and eventually manifest itself to being an "Effect" within our own personal "Existences" and "Experiences" . . . whether it be Fruit, Flowers, Weeds or Barren Landscapes! Bill highly regards the Fruits of his Labor and wishes that everyone would thus go on to plant "Lovely" Seeds on "Good Ground" in their own Gardens of Life!

to connect with Bill, he is all things Inner Child

www.iaminnerchild.com

Personal Web Site

www.iamjustbill.com

Imru' al-Qais bin Hujr al-Kindi

By way of the word,
I poetically ushered in
The wave of Arabic poetry & Poets
Who were to come

I left footprints
In the garden
Of which I had many.

I am a Bedoin,
I am a King
One whom even
The Prophet Muhammad (PBUH)
Paid homage

My words had meaning then
As much as they do now

I encouraged the wind
To whisper to the souls of men
And they have been inspired
For centuries past
And centuries to come

Come taste of my verse,
It is a sweet inebriating wine
Like the nectar of the Gods,
For his angels
Spoke to my soul
As I speak to you . . .
Hark, listen,
I am
Imru' al-Qais bin Hujr al-Kindi

Alchemist

With just a little hope,

And some well positioned dreams,

A bucket full of will,

And a heart full of humanity,

And we can change the world!

1 eye blind

A deep rose colored monocle
Adorns the left,
The right?

Night endures
Sight obscures
There are no sure- ities
That appease our wonder
Our quest
For truth

The test we face
Has a space ... somewhere
Out there in the nefarious ether,
The never ever neither either
Where you nor I
Can seem to get to

The anguish
Of no light,
Only blight seen
Demeans our essence,
But our very presence
Confirms the present,
Yet to come,
And validates our delusion
Pertaining the illusion s
Of the past
And the future
We must face ...
Can you taste
Your sense of it all

Worry not
About the fall,
For it has already happened
And perhaps ...
We are flapping
Broken wings
Attempting to fly
In the liquid soup
Of subterfugeous dischord

1 eye blind,
The other adorns
A deeply colored
Rose flavored monocle

Smell the flowers my child
Smell the flowers,
For therein lies
The hope you have yet
To grasp.

Poke me in my 3rd eye,
And perchance
I will know you are here
With me

December 2024 Featured Poets

Kapardeli Eftichia

Irena Jovanović

Sudipta Mishra

Til Kumari Sharma

Kapardeli Eftichia

Kapardeli Eftichia – From Greece has a degree as an art conservator 2021 She has a Doctorate from **Arts And Culture World Academy**. World Academy of Art and Culture | Facebook *International Ambassador of the International Chamber of Writers and Artists LIC ,Member of* **the World Poets' society** *and* **poetas del mundo** *, member of the IWA, member of Ε.Ε.Λ.Σ.Π.Η* **The Union of Greek Writers - Authors of the Five Continents,** *member of the* **International Society Of Greek Literatures – Artists - Deel** *and* **Pel** *(the world association of writers in Greece) Panhellenic Union of Writers.*

http://eftichiakapa.blogspot.gr/2013_10_01_archive.html

ΑΓΟΝΕΣ ΓΡΑΜΜΕΣ

Άγονες γραμμές γεμάτες ταξίδια
άγονες γραμμές χωρίς αγκαλιές
 οι σκιές μας μοιρασμένες
οι διαδρομές μας πετρωμένες
και οι ρίζες μας κομμένες

Άγονες γραμμές ,απολιθωμένες
σε συνθήκες ματαιωμένες
σε μέρες που τρυπούν και κολλούν
στο σώμα με πνοές, ματωμένες

Έρημη χώρα η ζωή μας
πάντα θρηνεί την αποχώρηση μας
 και για τα βελούδινα αγγίγματα θρηνεί
που στριμωγμένα ,σε ασταθή
ορίζοντα βυθίζονται ,μοιάζουν αγριολούλουδα ξεριζωμένα
στο πλήθος για μένα και για σένα

Στην κούραση άνθρωποι σμίγουν ,μας μιλούν
και με γυμνά βρεγμένα χέρια μας χαιρετούν στην άμορφη
μάζα των χρόνων με την Ηχώ της Άρνησης ,στα φώτα της
Πόλης που
στολίζουν τα σπίτια και τις κάμαρες
μας προσπερνούν

Infertile lines

Infertile lines full of travel
Infertile lines without hugs
  our routes are stony ,our roots,
cut off and
our shadows, are divided

Infertile lines, petrified
in aborted conditions
on days that pierce and stick
in the body with breaths, bloody

Our life is a desert country
always mourns our departure
  and for the velvet touches he mourns
that squished, in unstable
horizon they sink, they look like wild flowers uprooted
in the crowd, for me and you

In fatigue, people come together,
they talk to us
and with bare wet hands they greet us
in the formless mass of the years
with the Echo of Denial, in the lights of the City that
they decorate houses and chambers
they pass us

Μητερα Γη

Στην χρυσή κοιλάδα με τον απέραντο ουρανό
στη γη της αθωότητας
Εκεί που τα σύννεφα της σκόνης
έλιωναν στο φώς του Ήλιου
Εκεί που το νερό του ποταμού
σκέπαζε τα γυμνό μου σώμα με τα μυστικά και τα χαμόγελα
όλου του κόσμου
Και ένα πανέμορφο λουλούδι
σπόρος της μάνας γης ,στις ρίζες ενός δένδρου
να με καλεί ……………εκεί
Και τώρα η καταστροφή , η εισβολή ,η ρύπανση
Κόκκινη γη …τα θεμέλια σου σκάβουν
άσχημοι καιροί ,και τα σπλάχνα σου καίουν
στάχτη και σκόνη ,ζώα φοβισμένα
ρίζες νεκρές, έρημα τα βουνά ,η ζέστη το χώμα καίει
Οι μηλιές δεν θα έχουν πια καρπούς ,το τριαντάφυλλο δεν θα
ανοίξει πια
οι μελωδίες θα έχουν σιωπήσει, με κουρασμένα και νεκρά πουλιά
Και το δένδρο ,που αλλάζει
κάθε εποχή θα μας προσκαλεί να ταξιδέψουμε
με τα φύλλα που του πήρε ο άνεμος την αυγή
Στην ψυχρή σιωπή και την καταδίκη
στην αγκαλιά μου αργοπεθαίνει
Η πρώτη αγαπημένη μου μητέρα ,η Γη

Mother Earth

In the golden valley with the vast sky
in the land of innocence
Where the clouds of dust
melted in the light of the Sun.
Where the river water
covered my naked body with secrets and smiles
of the whole world
And a beautiful flower
seed of mother earth, at the roots of a tree
to call me ……………. .there
And now the destruction, the invasion, the pollution
Red earth, your foundations are digging
bad times, and your bowels are burning
ash and dust, scared animals
roots dead, mountains deserted, heat the soil burns
The apple trees will no longer bear fruit, the rose will no longer
open
the melodies will be silent, with tired and dead birds
And the tree, which changes
every season will invite us to travel
with the leaves that the wind took at dawn
In cold silence and condemnation
in my arms he dies late
My first beloved mother, Earth

Irena Jovanović

Irena Jovanović

Irena Jovanović from Zaječar, Serbia (born in 1971) is a Master of Ceramics Design, Painter and Poetess. She has been writing poetry since 1992, and has published her poetry book „Let It Be" with „Inner Child Press" in USA in 2013. She writes poetry both in Serbian and in English, and publishes in online magazines, Facebook groups, and her Facebook page, as well as in printed magazines in her country and abroad. She founded a club for poetesses in her hometown and is leading it, with 30 members of different ages, and poetry reading once in a week.

Being Interconnected

With nature and universe
with energies and dimensions
with particles and transcendence
with vibrations and fractals
with Fibonacci Sequence and Golden Ratio
with mandalas and water memories
with cells, atoms, and subatomic domain
with frequencies and creation
with sun, earth, wind, oceans
moon, planets, synchronicity and all
with soul and Supreme soul
it's natural to be
interconnected
with universal codes and ciphers
with ancient secrets and mysteries
with crystals, rocks, depth and eons
with timelessness, eternity, bliss and endlessness
with vastness of ideas of the most brilliant mind
with essence, substance, purpose and cause
with everything possible and impossible at all
with life, change, continuity and path
it is absolutely primordial
to be interconnected
with sacred geometry and perfect miracles
with DNA sequences and infinite knowledge
with inner silences and immersive meditations
with fluffy snowflake images
and interstellar travels
and all knots-woven patterns and plans
blueprints, schemes and schedules
with time and space, events and stillness
with gods, deities, sacredness and truth

yes, it is very much and positively recommended
to be opened and highly perceptive
it is very good, very best and exquisite
it is extraordinarily majestic indeed
being in tune, being in harmony
being in tao
being interconnected

Irena Jovanović

Both Heaven And Nature Sing

Uplifted vibrations of brilliant whiteness
purity in perfect, essential
crystal clear shiny eloquence
of winter wise covers
making all nature sleep and rest
in preparation for new life burst
for spring of joy
now meditating so deeply, inside
planning, dreaming, getting all ready
for the next brand new motion
play, performance, interpretation
during and throughout
this snow-white intermezzo
in orchestration of
exceptional life symphony
now singing in mind and soul
high frequencies on sky and ground
everywhere
so pleasing
so neat and delightful
so unlimited
so fulfilling, so blissful
oneiric
both heaven and nature intone
this ultimate melody of whiteness
within the clear mind
of ultimate creature…
…creating universe choruses…
of eternal whiteness…
within sound…
vibrating…

Emerald Gardens

Evergreen thoughts
deeply diving into the Self
recalling peaceful nuances
and mildest waves of the attitude
of the natural and wild growth echoes
listening to miraculous interiors
entering emerald gardens of the mind
finding tender bliss and openness
to the widest ranges of endlessness
of eternity of our soul residing
in green areas of a heart garden
energy beautiful as an unreal dream
as an unchangeable fairy tale
very brilliant part of a being
in any circumstances present
and all present in the glory of God
laid down in a true beauty
in emerald gardens
set just for its throne
presiding over all appearances
offering brilliance unconditionally
harmonizing each and every move
leading all to the light of the substance
residing in absolute undivided fantasy of joy
unimaginable realms of utmost experience
wonderful, ecstatic, ravishing, astonishing
in emerald gardens
of Lord's dreams…

Irena Jovanović

Sudipta Mishra

Sudipta Mishra

Sudipta Mishra is a multi-faceted artist and dancer. She has weaved more than a hundred books, as a coauthor. Her third book, 'The Essence of Life', is credited with Amazon's best seller, and her next book, 'The Songs of My Heart' is scaling newer heights of glory. She garnered numerous accolades from international literary organizations like the famous Rabindranath Tagore Memorial, Mahadevi Verma Sahitya Siromani Award, Powerful Women Award, and so on. She regularly pens articles in newspapers as a strong female voice against gender discrimination, global warming, domestic violence against women, etc. She is pursuing a PhD degree in English at Jaipur, India.

Ennui

Oh! I have to walk again
on the known valleys of tedium
"I am bored now and that's all"

The same sunshine penetrated my skin
Giving me a sign of living
Again the sun has drowned in the wide unknown

With the soft murmurs from leaves
I realize the ritual of the flock of birds
Fluttering, silky wings disappear in the sky

Soaring desires tempt me to live
Crowded streets chase me with desolate appetites
I peep into the empty houses

No more I can see the laughing walls
What is left there?
Corpses of dead desires hang on the roof

I can see hunger, there
The cravings for love succumb to a realm of nothingness
A cycle continues

Desperation settles everywhere
Clouds of fear cover the sky
I silently sip my tears

I submit my empty wishes
Upon the arrival of a new day
Again I try to hold the hands of Ennui...

The Mute Doll

There was a doll, so beautiful
pretty eyes and lovely lips
Then came a man
Master in the art of stagecraft
He played with the puppet
The dummy obeyed its master
Everything went well
The magic was lauded by all
The roly-poly toy became everyone's favorite

In the World of Deception,
The doll played so well
It swayed with the blowing air
Never did it disobey the commands
It rose to fame
With golden wings
To touch the sky
Suddenly the strings were cut
The master died
Now, the doll was in foul hands
The dumb doll failed to listen to the multiple voices
Nobody loved the voiceless, poor fellow
Now, the mute doll is left in a glass case
With drooping eyes,
it greets everyone at the doorstep
Nodding its head in a slightly tilted face!

Ignorance

I do not know the reason
I can only hear a voice inside me
My soul sings a poem, so pure
so melodic, stirring
A song that speaks the voice of silence
That ripples inside my chest
Sparkling ideas boil in my mind
I just form them and
I whisper them in the spiraling wind
For reaching out to you all

I console and negotiate with words
My untamed mind always struggle
To express my conflicting feelings
Finally, words explore the game
In the game of intriguing thoughts,
I cajole my verses to note my expression!
Oh, then the weight of my memory
Finds a subtle way to release...

Til Kumari Sharma

Til Kumari Sharma

Til Kumari Sharma was born in Hile, Paiyun 7, Parbat, Nepal. She is known as Pushpa too. Her parents are Mr. Hari Prasad Basel Sharma (Mayor of Village Assembly in the time of Kingdom) and Mrs. Liladevi Bhusal Bashyal. Her PhD is in English Literature from Singhania University in Rajasthan, India. She has published many thousands of poems, some essays, stories and other literary writings from Nepal, Russia, America, England, Scotland, Indonesia, Bangladesh, South Africa, Kenya, North Africa, Trinidad and Tobago, Spain, India and others. She is co- author in best-selling anthologies.

WhatsApp: + 9779749497960
Email: authortilks@gmail.com

Alienated Life Journey

The birth alone is our life.
Death alone is our journey to reach.
Destiny of everybody is to reach in death bed.
No alive ness is eternal here.
Body melts in soil.
Bone acts as light of earth.
Nothing has complete death in real world.
Transformation is essential.
The birth and death are enemies and friends.
The womb of mother is tomb too.
It has already structured tomb in womb.
So birth meets life in tomb.
The harmony is death too.
Loss is gain too.
Death is guest to take life.
Again it brings birth of someone.
Soul is taking journey.
Spirit has friendship with air and wind.
Storm is my breath to defeat death.
Life is in journey of death.

Human Agony

The rope of agony is part of life.
Smiling is another part of life.
The essence is to breathe.
The alive ness is our acting in theatre.
The dancing is our movement.
The light is to see death.
Pyre is our destination.
It is eternal home.
It is light of life.
The duty is to regard happiness.
Smiling is an art of agony.
Tears are blocking happiness.
The happiness is brief and short.
Grief is built up of human agony.
The walls of life are higher.
Genuine beauty is lost in agony.
To grieve is essence of life.
Agony is in the end of life.

Harmony of Humanity

Humanity as light in earth.
It is inborn in particular human.
The delighting is in humanity in world.
Human is higher being in earth.
Consciousness is our heart with mind.
Humanity in world is huge achievement.
The harmony is ornament.
That leads world of moral wisdom.
The association of world people is humanity in earth.
The alienated selfishness is mad point.

Considering other is huge tribute.
The life is decorated with cloth of humanity.
Then world is our home.
No boarder in our friendship is in humanity of world.
The wonder is the human discrimination.
Humanity does not like discrimination.
Love with humanity is our jewel of harmony.
The gist of life is to help each other with respect.

Remembering

our fallen soldiers of verse

Janet Perkins Caldwell
February 14, 1959 ~ September 20, 2016

Alan W. Jankowski
16 March 1961 ~ 10 March 2017

The Butterfly Effect

"IS" in effect

Inner Child Press News

Published Books by Poetry Posse Members

We are so excited to share and announce a few of the current books, as well as the new and upcoming books of some of our Poetry Posse authors.

On the following pages we present to you ...

Inner Child Press News

Alicja Maria Kuberska
Jackie Davis Allen
Gail Weston Shazor
hülya n. yılmaz
Nizar Sartawi
Elizabeth E. Castillo
Faleeha Hassan
Fahredin Shehu
Kimberly Burnham
Caroline 'Ceri' Nazareno
Eliza Segiet
Teresa E. Gallion
Mutawaf Shaheed
William S. Peters, Sr.

Now Available

www.innerchildpress.com

The Year of the Poet XI ~ December 2024

Now Available
www.innerchildpress.com

Inner Child Press News

Now Available
www.innerchildpress.com

Now Available
www.innerchildpress.com

Now Available
www.innerchildpress.com

The Year of the Poet XI ~ December 2024

Now Available
www.innerchildpress.com

Inner Child Press News

Now Available
www.innerchildpress.com

The Year of the Poet XI ~ December 2024

Now Available
www.innerchildpress.com

Inner Child Press News

Now Available
www.innerchildpress.com

The Year of the Poet XI ~ December 2024

Pulling Coats

Shareef Abdur-Rasheed

Now Available
www.innerchildpress.com

Now Available
www.innerchildpress.com

The Year of the Poet XI ~ December 2024

Alicja Maria Kuberska

Now Available
www.innerchildpress.com

Inner Child Press News

Now Available
www.innerchildpress.com

The Year of the Poet XI ~ December 2024

Now Available
www.innerchildpress.com

Inner Child Press News

Now Available at
www.innerchildpress.com

The Year of the Poet XI ~ December 2024

Now Available at
www.amazon.com/gp/product/B08MYL5B7S/ref=
dbs_a_def_rwt_hsch_vapi_tkin_p1_i2

Inner Child Press News

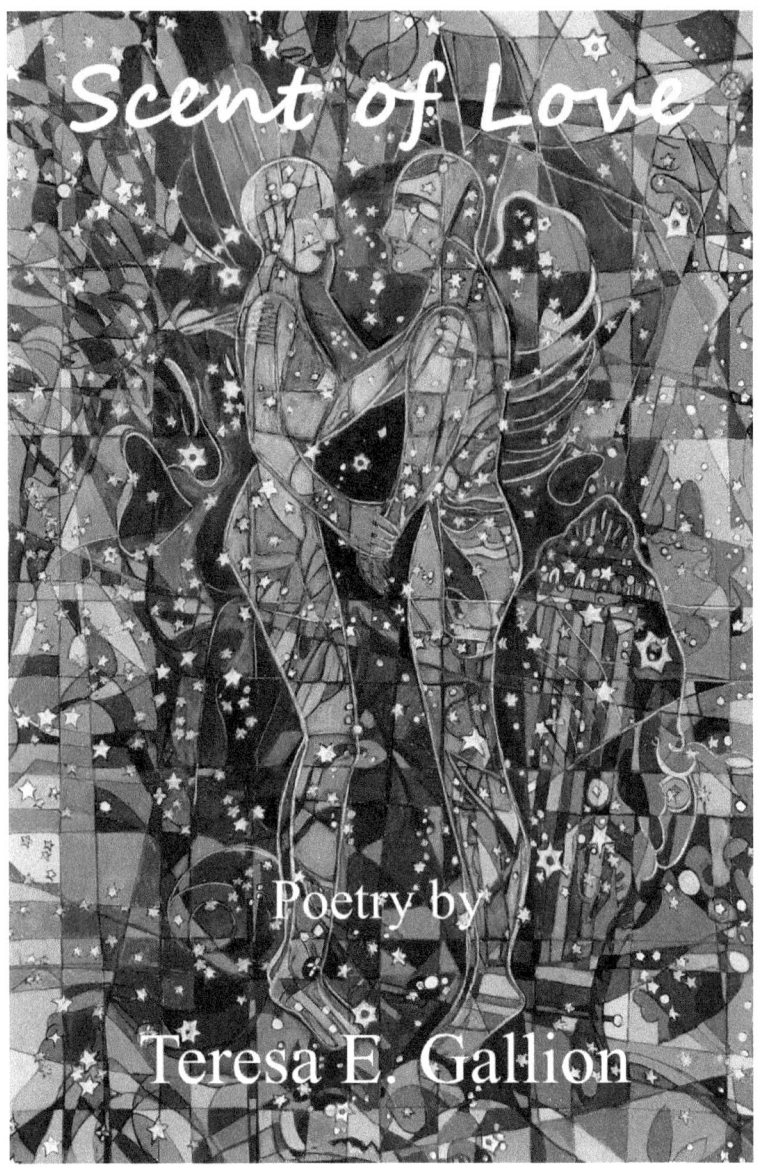

Now Available
www.innerchildpress.com

The Year of the Poet XI ~ December 2024

Now Available
www.innerchildpress.com

Inner Child Press News

Now Available
www.innerchildpress.com

The Year of the Poet XI ~ December 2024

Now Available
www.innerchildpress.com

Now Available
www.innerchildpress.com

The Year of the Poet XI ~ December 2024

Now Available
www.innerchildpress.com

Now Available
www.innerchildpress.com

Now Available
www.innerchildpress.com

Inner Child Press News

Now Available
www.innerchildpress.com

The Year of the Poet XI ~ December 2024

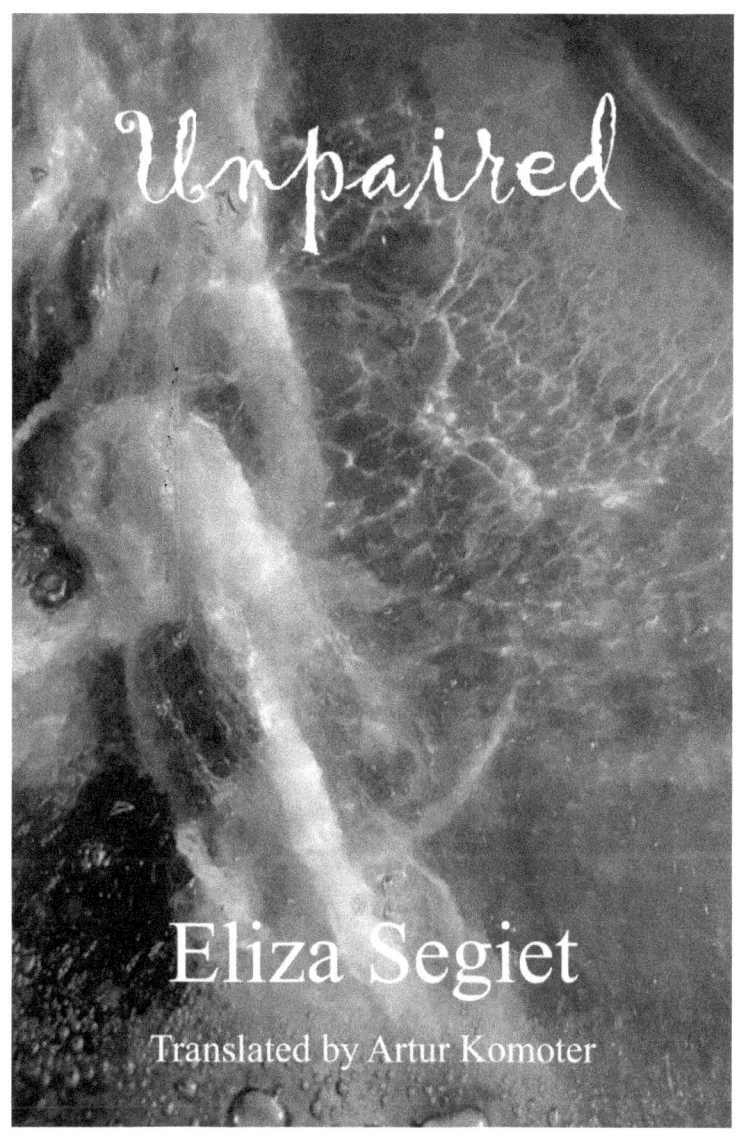

Private Issue
www.innerchildpress.com

Inner Child Press News

Now Available
www.innerchildpress.com

The Year of the Poet XI ~ December 2024

Butterfly's Voice

Faleeha Hassan

Translated by William M. Hutchins

Now Available at
www.innerchildpress.com

Inner Child Press News

Now Available at
www.innerchildpress.com

The Year of the Poet XI ~ December 2024

Now Available at
www.innerchildpress.com

Now Available at
www.innerchildpress.com

The Year of the Poet XI ~ December 2024

HERENOW

FAHREDIN SHEHU

Now Available at
www.innerchildpress.com

Inner Child Press News

Now Available at
www.innerchildpress.com

The Year of the Poet XI ~ December 2024

Now Available at
www.innerchildpress.com

Inner Child Press News

Now Available at
www.innerchildpress.com

The Year of the Poet XI ~ December 2024

Now Available at
www.innerchildpress.com

Inner Child Press News

Now Available at
www.innerchildpress.com

The Year of the Poet XI ~ December 2024

Breakfast for Butterflies

Faleeha Hassan

Now Available at
www.innerchildpress.com

Inner Child Press News

Now Available at
www.innerchildpress.com

The Year of the Poet XI ~ December 2024

Now Available at
www.innerchildpress.com

Inner Child Press News

Now Available at
www.innerchildpress.com

Inner Child Press News

Now Available
www.innerchildpress.com

Other Anthological works from

Inner Child Press International

www.innerchildpress.com

Inner Child Press Anthologies

Now Available
www.worldhealingworldpeacepoetry.com

Inner Child Press Anthologies

Now Available
www.worldhealingworldpeacepoetry.com

Inner Child Press Anthologies

Now Available
www.worldhealingworldpeacepoetry.com

Inner Child Press Anthologies

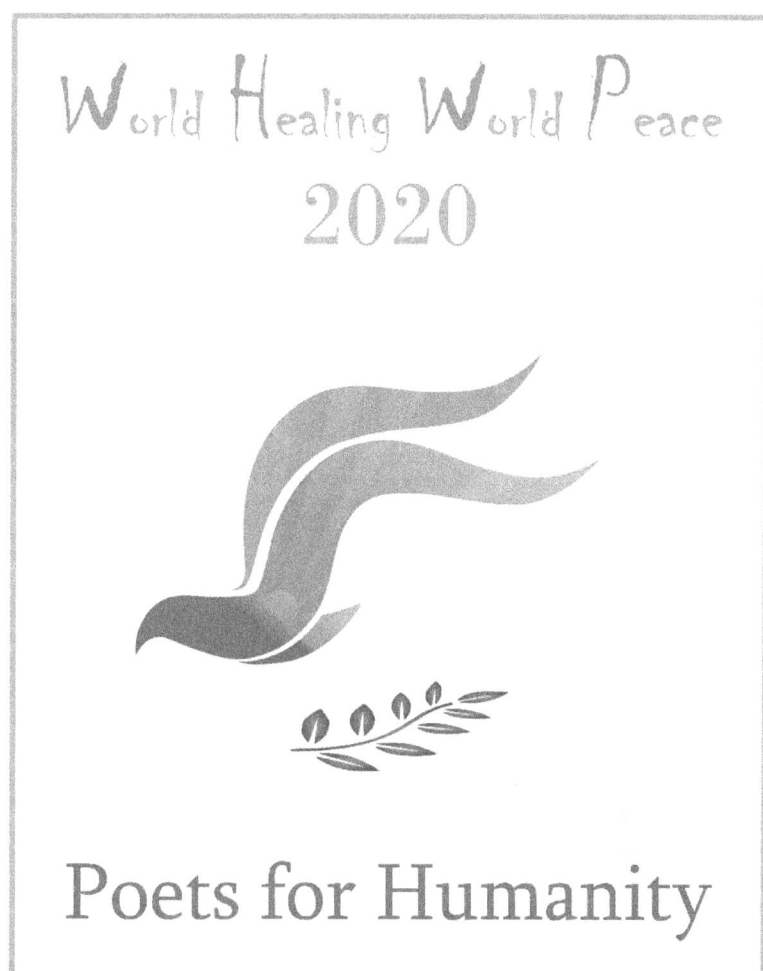

Now Available
www.worldhealingworldpeacepoetry.com

Inner Child Press Anthologies

Now Available
www.innerchildpress.com

Inner Child Press Anthologies

Inner Child Press International
&
The Year of the Poet
present

Poetry
the best of 2020

Poets of the World

Now Available
www.innerchildpress.com

Inner Child Press Anthologies

Now Available
www.innerchildpress.com

Inner Child Press Anthologies

Now Available
www.innerchildpress.com

Inner Child Press Anthologies

Now Available
www.innerchildpress.com

Inner Child Press Anthologies

Now Available at
www.innerchildpress.com

Inner Child Press Anthologies

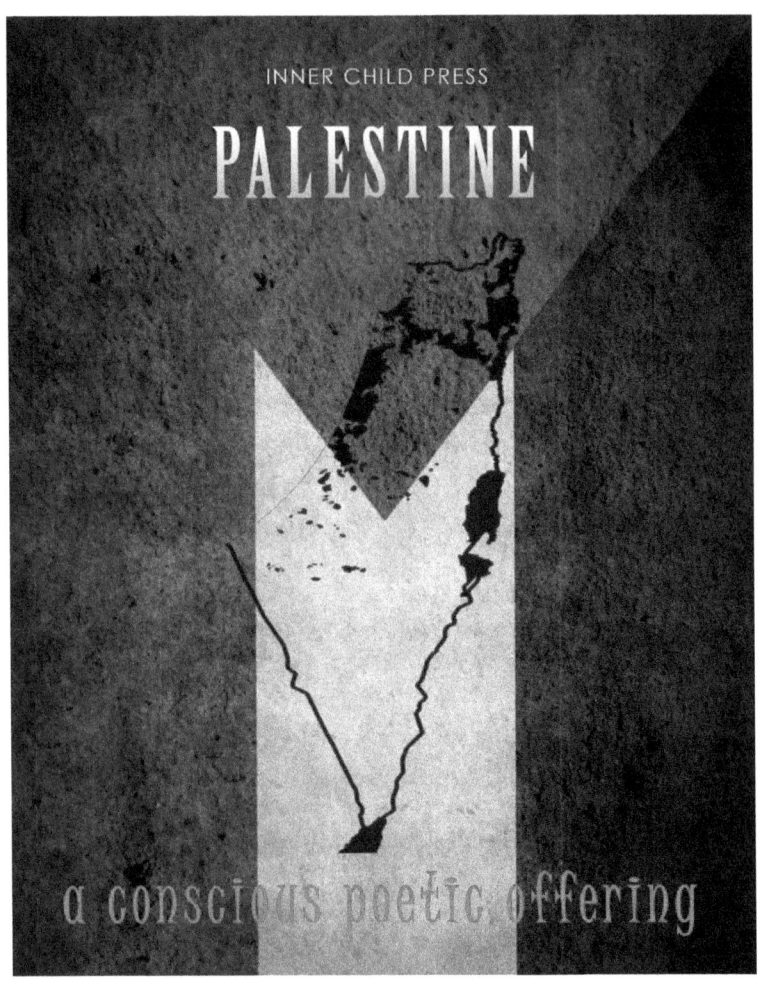

Now Available at
www.innerchildpress.com

Inner Child Press Anthologies

Now Available at
www.innerchildpress.com

Inner Child Press Anthologies

Now Available
www.worldhealingworldpeacepoetry.com

Inner Child Press Anthologies

Now Available
www.worldhealingworldpeacepoetry.com

Inner Child Press Anthologies

Now Available
www.worldhealingworldpeacepoetry.com

Inner Child Press Anthologies

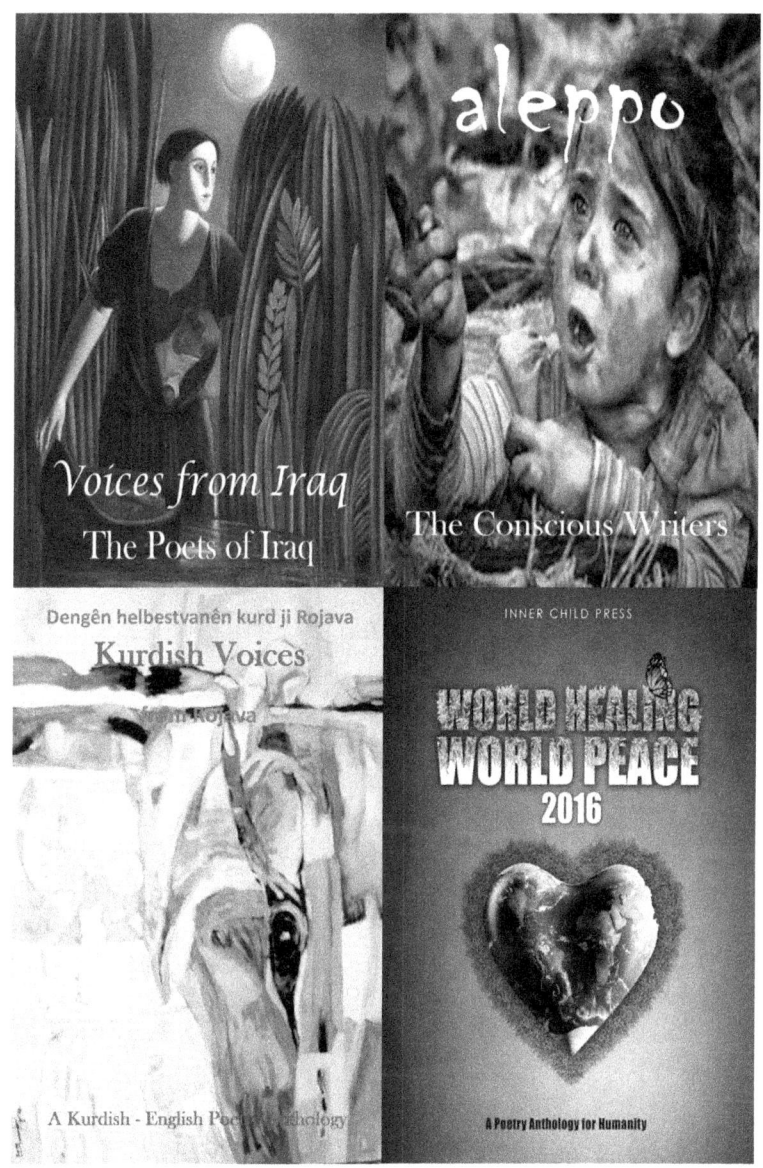

Now Available
www.innerchildpress.com/anthologies

Inner Child Press Anthologies

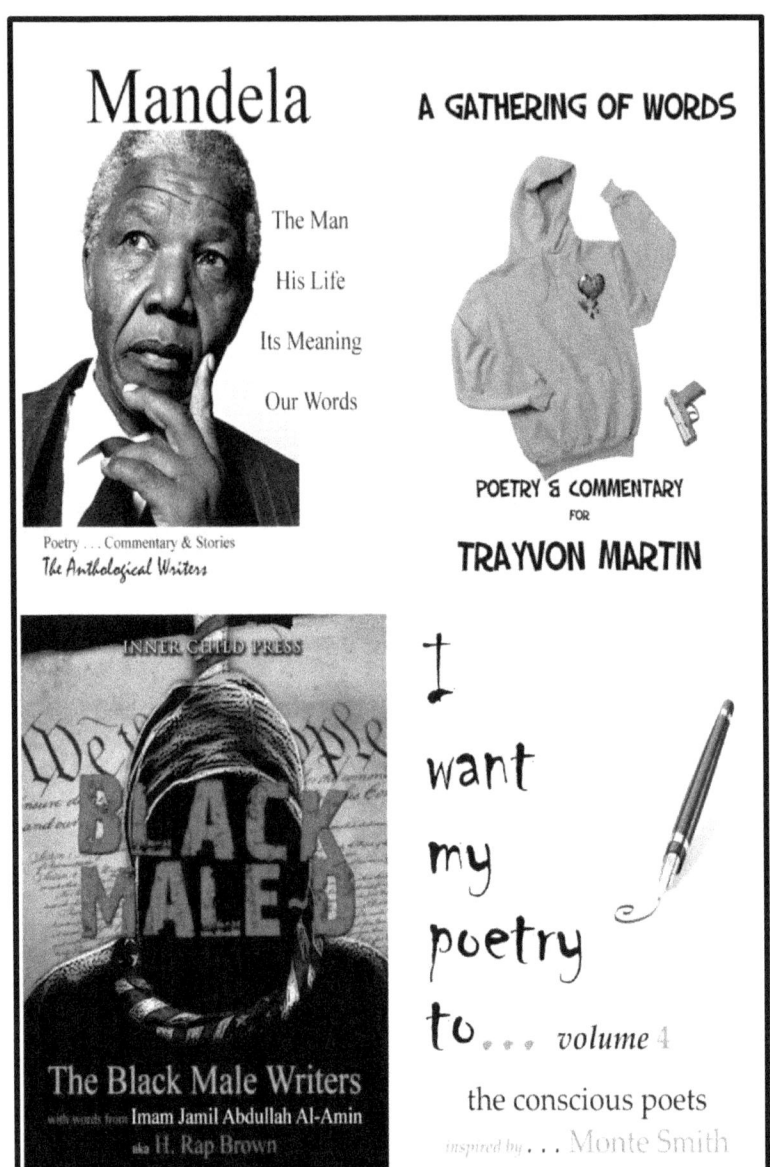

Now Available
www.innerchildpress.com/anthologies

Inner Child Press Anthologies

Now Available
www.innerchildpress.com/anthologies

Inner Child Press Anthologies

Now Available
www.innerchildpress.com/anthologies

Inner Child Press Anthologies

Now Available
www.innerchildpress.com/anthologies

Inner Child Press Anthologies

Now Available
www.innerchildpress.com/the-year-of-the-poet

Inner Child Press Anthologies

Now Available

www.innerchildpress.com/the-year-of-the-poet

Inner Child Press Anthologies

Now Available
www.innerchildpress.com/the-year-of-the-poet

Inner Child Press Anthologies

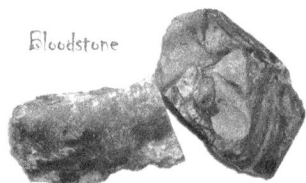

Now Available
www.innerchildpress.com/the-year-of-the-poet

Inner Child Press Anthologies

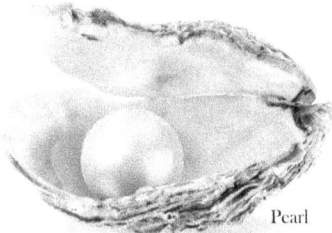
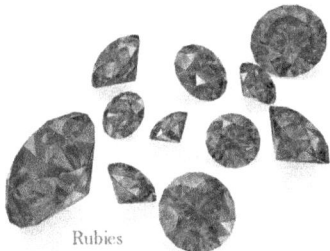

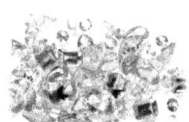

Now Available
www.innerchildpress.com/the-year-of-the-poet

Inner Child Press Anthologies

Now Available
www.innerchildpress.com/the-year-of-the-poet

Inner Child Press Anthologies

Now Available
www.innerchildpress.com/the-year-of-the-poet

Inner Child Press Anthologies

Now Available

www.innerchildpress.com/the-year-of-the-poet

Inner Child Press Anthologies

Now Available
www.innerchildpress.com/the-year-of-the-poet

Inner Child Press Anthologies

Now Available
www.innerchildpress.com/the-year-of-the-poet

Inner Child Press Anthologies

Now Available

www.innerchildpress.com/the-year-of-the-poet

Inner Child Press Anthologies

The Year of the Poet IV
September 2017

Featured Poets
Martina Reisz Newberry
Ameer Nassir
Christine Fulco Neal
Robert Neal

The Elm Tree

The Poetry Posse 2017

Gail Weston Shazor * Caroline Nazareno * Bismay Mohanty
Teresa E. Gallion * Anna Jakubczak Vel Ratty Adalan
Joe DaVerbal Minddancer * Shareef Abdur – Rasheed
Albert Carrasco * Kimberly Burnham * Elizabeth Castillo
Hülya N. Yılmaz * Faleeha Hassan * Jackie Davis Allen
Jen Walls * Nizar Sartawi * William S. Peters, Sr.

The Year of the Poet IV
October 2017

Featured Poets
Ahmed Abu Saleem
Nedal Al-Qaeim
Sadeddin Shahin

The Black Walnut Tree

The Poetry Posse 2017

Gail Weston Shazor * Caroline Nazareno * Bismay Mohanty
Teresa E. Gallion * Anna Jakubczak Vel Ratty Adalan
Joe DaVerbal Minddancer * Shareef Abdur – Rasheed
Albert Carrasco * Kimberly Burnham * Elizabeth Castillo
Hülya N. Yılmaz * Faleeha Hassan * Jackie Davis Allen
Jen Walls * Nizar Sartawi * * William S. Peters, Sr.

The Year of the Poet IV
November 2017

Featured Poets
Kay Peters
Alfreda D. Ghee
Gabriella Garofalo
Rosemary Cappello

The Tree of Life

The Poetry Posse 2017

Gail Weston Shazor * Caroline Nazareno * Bismay Mohanty
Teresa E. Gallion * Anna Jakubczak Vel Ratty Adalan
Joe DaVerbal Minddancer * Shareef Abdur – Rasheed
Albert Carrasco * Kimberly Burnham * Elizabeth Castillo
Hülya N. Yılmaz * Faleeha Hassan * Jackie Davis Allen
Jen Walls * Nizar Sartawi * William S. Peters, Sr.

The Year of the Poet IV
December 2017

Featured Poets
Justice Clarke
Mariel M. Pabroa
Kiley Brown

The Fig Tree

The Poetry Posse 2017

Gail Weston Shazor * Caroline Nazareno * Bismay Mohanty
Teresa E. Gallion * Anna Jakubczak Vel Ratty Adalan
Joe DaVerbal Minddancer * Shareef Abdur – Rasheed
Albert Carrasco * Kimberly Burnham * Elizabeth Castillo
Hülya N. Yılmaz * Faleeha Hassan * Jackie Davis Allen
Jen Walls * Nizar Sartawi * William S. Peters, Sr.

Now Available
www.innerchildpress.com/the-year-of-the-poet

Inner Child Press Anthologies

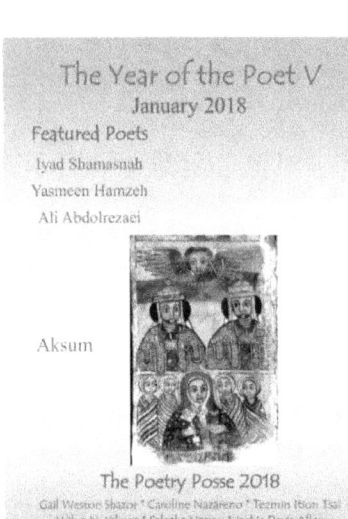

Now Available
www.innerchildpress.com/the-year-of-the-poet

Inner Child Press Anthologies

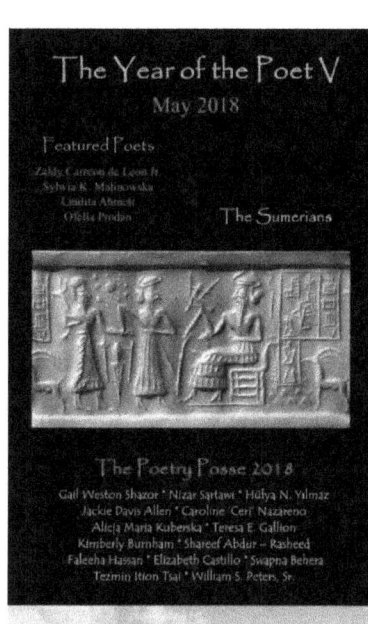
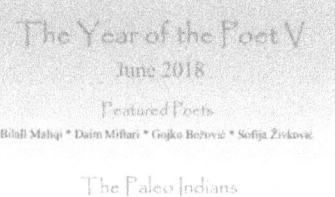

Now Available
www.innerchildpress.com/the-year-of-the-poet

Inner Child Press Anthologies

Now Available
www.innerchildpress.com/the-year-of-the-poet

Inner Child Press Anthologies

The Year of the Poet VI
January 2019

Indigenous North Americans

Featured Poets
Houda Elfchtali
Anthony Briscoe
Iram Fatima 'Ashi'
Dr. K. K. Mathew

Dream Catcher

The Poetry Posse 2019

The Year of the Poet VI
February 2019

Featured Poets
Marek Lukaszewicz * Bharati Nayak
Aida G. Roque * Jean-Jacques Fournier

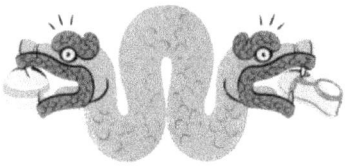

Meso-America

The Poetry Posse 2019

The Year of the Poet VI
March 2019

Featured Poets
Eniesa Mahmic * Sylwia K. Malinowska
Shurouk Hammoud * Anwer Ghani

The Caribbean

The Year of the Poet VI
April 2019

Featured Poets
DL Davis * Michelle Joan Barulich
Lulëzim Haziri * Faleeha Hassan

Central & West Africa

The Poetry Posse 2019

Gail Weston Shazor * Albert Carrasco * Hülya N. Yılmaz
Jackie Davis Allen * Caroline Nazareno * Eliza Segiet
Alicja Maria Kubenska * Teresa E. Gallion * Joe Paire
Kimberly Burnham * Shareef Abdur - Rasheed
Ashok K. Bhargava * Elizabeth Castillo * Swapna Behera
Tezmin Ition Tsai * William S. Peters, Sr

Now Available
www.innerchildpress.com/the-year-of-the-poet

237

Inner Child Press Anthologies

Now Available
www.innerchildpress.com/the-year-of-the-poet

Inner Child Press Anthologies

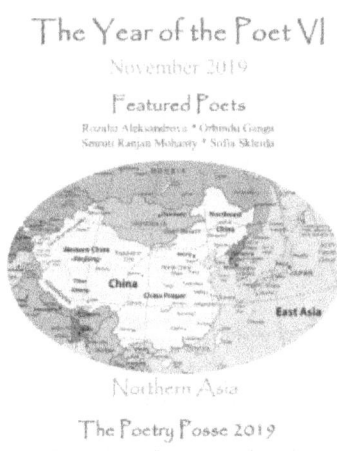

Now Available
www.innerchildpress.com/the-year-of-the-poet

Inner Child Press Anthologies

Now Available

www.innerchildpress.com/the-year-of-the-poet

Inner Child Press Anthologies

Now Available
www.innerchildpress.com/the-year-of-the-poet

Inner Child Press Anthologies

Now Available
www.innerchildpress.com/the-year-of-the-poet

Inner Child Press Anthologies

The Year of the Poet VIII
January 2021

Featured Global Poets
Andrew Scott * Debaprasanna Biswas
Shakil Kalam * Changming Yuan

Banksy's The Girl with the Pierced Eardrum

Poetry . . . Ekphrasticly Speaking
The Poetry Posse 2020

Gail Weston Shazor * Albert Carasco * Hülya N. Yılmaz
Jackie Davis Allen * Caroline Nazareno * Eliza Segiet
Alicja Maria Kuberska * Teresa E. Gallion * Joe Paire
Kimberly Burnham * Shareef Abdur - Rasheed
Ashok K. Bhargava * Elizabeth Castillo * Swapna Behera
Tezmin Ition Tsai * William S. Peters, Sr.

The Year of the Poet VIII
February 2021

Featured Global Poets
T. Ramesh Babu * Ruchida Barman
Neptune Barman * Faleeha Hassan

Emory Douglas : 1968 Olympics mural

Poetry . . . Ekphrasticly Speaking
The Poetry Posse 2021

Gail Weston Shazor * Albert Carasco * Hülya N. Yılmaz
Jackie Davis Allen * Caroline Nazareno * Eliza Segiet
Alicja Maria Kuberska * Teresa E. Gallion * Joe Paire
Kimberly Burnham * Shareef Abdur - Rasheed
Ashok K. Bhargava * Elizabeth Castillo * Swapna Behera
Tezmin Ition Tsai * William S. Peters, Sr.

The Year of the Poet VIII
March 2021

Featured Global Poets
Claudia Piccinno * Mohammed Jabr
Luzviminda Rivera * Nigar Arif

Tatyana Fazlalizadeh

Poetry . . . Ekphrasticly Speaking
The Poetry Posse 2021

Gail Weston Shazor * Albert Carasco * Hülya N. Yılmaz
Jackie Davis Allen * Caroline Nazareno * Eliza Segiet
Alicja Maria Kuberska * Teresa E. Gallion * Joe Paire
Kimberly Burnham * Shareef Abdur - Rasheed
Ashok K. Bhargava * Elizabeth Castillo * Swapna Behera
Tezmin Ition Tsai * William S. Peters, Sr.

The Year of the Poet VIII
April 2021

Featured Global Poets
Katarzyna Brus- Sawczuk * Anwesha Paul
Rozalia Aleksandrova * Shahid Abbas

Pablo O'Higgins

Poetry . . . Ekphrasticly Speaking
The Poetry Posse 2021

Gail Weston Shazor * Albert Carasco * Hülya N. Yılmaz
Jackie Davis Allen * Caroline Nazareno * Eliza Segiet
Alicja Maria Kuberska * Teresa E. Gallion * Joe Paire
Kimberly Burnham * Shareef Abdur - Rasheed
Ashok K. Bhargava * Elizabeth Castillo * Swapna Behera
Tezmin Ition Tsai * William S. Peters, Sr.

Now Available
www.innerchildpress.com/the-year-of-the-poet

Inner Child Press Anthologies

Now Available

www.innerchildpress.com/the-year-of-the-poet

Inner Child Press Anthologies

Now Available

www.innerchildpress.com/the-year-of-the-poet

Inner Child Press Anthologies

The Year of the Poet IX
January 2022

Featured Global Poets
**Ratan Ghosh * Christine Neil-Wright
Andrew Scott * Ashok Kumar**

Climate Change : The Ice Cap

Poetry . . . Ekphrasticly Speaking

The Poetry Posse 2021

Gail Weston Shazor * Albert Carassco * Hülya N. Yılmaz
Jackie Davis Allen * Caroline Nazareno * Eliza Segiet
Alicja Maria Kuberska * Teresa E. Gallion * Joe Paire
Kimberly Burnham * Shareef Abdur – Rasheed
Ashok K. Bhargava * Elizabeth Castillo * Swapna Behera
Tezmin Ition Tsai * William S. Peters, Sr.

The Year of the Poet IX
February 2022

Featured Global Poets
Roza Boyanova * Ramón de Jesús Núñez Duval
Mammad Ismayil * Tarana Turan Rahimli

Climate Change and Mountains

Poetry . . . Ekphrasticly Speaking

The Poetry Posse 2021

Gail Weston Shazor * Albert Carasso * Hülya N. Yılmaz
Jackie Davis Allen * Caroline Nazareno * Eliza Segiet
Alicja Maria Kuberska * Teresa E. Gallion * Joe Paire
Kimberly Burnham * Shareef Abdur – Rasheed
Ashok K. Bhargava * Elizabeth Castillo * Swapna Behera
Tezmin Ition Tsai * William S. Peters, Sr.

The Year of the Poet IX
March 2022

Featured Global Poets
Dimitris P. Kraniotis * Marlene Pasini
Kennedy Ochieng * Swayam Prashant

Climate Change and Space Debris

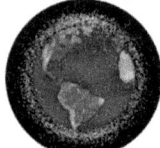

Poetry . . . Ekphrasticly Speaking

The Poetry Posse 2021

Gail Weston Shazor * Albert Carasso * Hülya N. Yılmaz
Jackie Davis Allen * Caroline Nazareno * Eliza Segiet
Alicja Maria Kuberska * Teresa E. Gallion * Joe Paire
Kimberly Burnham * Shareef Abdur – Rasheed
Ashok K. Bhargava * Elizabeth Castillo * Swapna Behera
Tezmin Ition Tsai * William S. Peters, Sr.

The Year of the Poet IX
April 2022

Featured Global Poets
**Alonzo Gross * Dr. Debaprasanna Biswas
Monsif Beroual * Carol Aronoff**

Climate Change and Oceans

Celebrating our 100th Edition

Poetry . . . Ekphrasticly Speaking

The Poetry Posse 2021

Gail Weston Shazor * Albert Carasso * Hülya N. Yılmaz
Jackie Davis Allen * Caroline Nazareno * Eliza Segiet
Alicja Maria Kuberska * Teresa E. Gallion * Joe Paire
Kimberly Burnham * Shareef Abdur – Rasheed
Ashok K. Bhargava * Elizabeth Castillo * Swapna Behera
Tezmin Ition Tsai * William S. Peters, Sr.

Now Available
www.innerchildpress.com/the-year-of-the-poet

Inner Child Press Anthologies

The Year of the Poet IX
May 2022

Featured Global Poets
Ndaba Sibanda * Smrutiranjan Mohanty
Ajanta Paul * Monalisa Dash Dwibedy

Climate Change and Birds

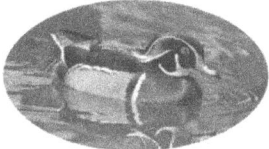

Poetry . . . Ekphrasticly Speaking

The Poetry Posse 2021

Gail Weston Shazor * Albert Carrasco * Hülya N. Yılmaz
Jackie Davis Allen * Caroline Nazareno * Eliza Segiet
Alicja Maria Kuberska * Teresa E. Gallion * Joe Paire
Kimberly Burnham * Shareef Abdur – Rasheed
Ashok K. Bhargava * Elizabeth Castillo * Swapna Behera
Tezmin Ition Tsai * William S. Peters, Sr.

The Year of the Poet IX
June 2022

Featured Global Poets
Yuan Changming * Azeezat Okunlola
Tanja Ajtić * Philip Chijioke Abonyi

Climate Change and Trees

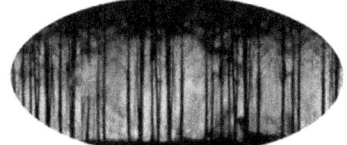

Poetry . . . Ekphrasticly Speaking

The Poetry Posse 2022

Gail Weston Shazor * Albert Carrasco * Hülya N. Yılmaz
Jackie Davis Allen * Caroline Nazareno * Eliza Segiet
Alicja Maria Kuberska * Teresa E. Gallion * Joe Paire
Kimberly Burnham * Shareef Abdur – Rasheed
Ashok K. Bhargava * Elizabeth Castillo * Swapna Behera
Tezmin Ition Tsai * William S. Peters, Sr.

The Year of the Poet IX
July 2022

Featured Global Poets
**Michelle Joan Barulich * Mili Das
Anna Ferriero * Ujjal Mandal**

Climate Change and Animals

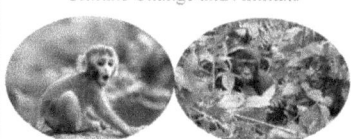

Poetry . . . Ekphrasticly Speaking

The Poetry Posse 2022

Gail Weston Shazor * Albert Carrasco * Hülya N. Yılmaz
Jackie Davis Allen * Caroline Nazareno * Eliza Segiet
Alicja Maria Kuberska * Teresa E. Gallion * Joe Paire
Kimberly Burnham * Shareef Abdur – Rasheed
Ashok K. Bhargava * Elizabeth Castillo * Swapna Behera
Tezmin Ition Tsai * William S. Peters, Sr.

The Year of the Poet IX
August 2022

Featured Global Poets
**Pankhuri Sinha * Abdulloh Abdumominov
Caroline Turunç * Tali Cohen Shabtai**

Climate Change and Agriculture

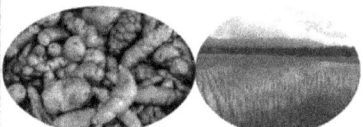

Poetry . . . Ekphrasticly Speaking

The Poetry Posse 2022

Gail Weston Shazor * Albert Carrasco * Hülya N. Yılmaz
Jackie Davis Allen * Caroline Nazareno * Eliza Segiet
Alicja Maria Kuberska * Teresa E. Gallion * Joe Paire
Kimberly Burnham * Shareef Abdur – Rasheed
Ashok K. Bhargava * Elizabeth Castillo * Swapna Behera
Tezmin Ition Tsai * William S. Peters, Sr.

Now Available
www.innerchildpress.com/the-year-of-the-poet

Inner Child Press Anthologies

The Year of the Poet IX
September 2022

Featured Global Poets

Ngozi Olivia Osuoha * Biswajit Mishra
Sylwia K. Malinowska * Sajid Hussein

Climate Change and Wind and Weather Patterns

Poetry … Ekphrasticly Speaking

The Poetry Posse 2022

Gail Weston Shazor * Albert Carasco * Hülya N. Yılmaz
Jackie Davis Allen * Caroline Nazareno * Eliza Segiet
Alicja Maria Kuberska * Teresa E. Gallion * Joe Paire
Kimberly Burnham * Shareef Abdur – Rasheed
Ashok K. Bhargava * Elizabeth Castillo * Swapna Behera
Tezmin Ition Tsai * William S. Peters, Sr.

The Year of the Poet IX
October 2022

Featured Global Poets

Andrew Kouroupos * Brenda Mohammed
Carthornia Kouroupos * Faleeha Hassan

Climate Change and Oil and Power

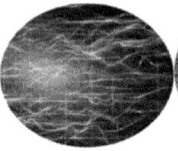 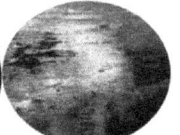

Poetry … Ekphrasticly Speaking

The Poetry Posse 2022

Gail Weston Shazor * Albert Carasco * Hülya N. Yılmaz
Jackie Davis Allen * Caroline Nazareno * Eliza Segiet
Alicja Maria Kuberska * Teresa E. Gallion * Joe Paire
Kimberly Burnham * Shareef Abdur – Rasheed
Ashok K. Bhargava * Elizabeth Castillo * Swapna Behera
Tezmin Ition Tsai * William S. Peters, Sr.

The Year of the Poet IX
November 2022

Featured Global Poets

Hema Ravi * Shafkat Aziz Hajam
Selma Kopic * Ibrahim Honjo

Climate Change : Time to Act

Poetry … Ekphrasticly Speaking

The Poetry Posse 2022

Gail Weston Shazor * Albert Carasco * Hülya N. Yılmaz
Jackie Davis Allen * Caroline Nazareno * Eliza Segiet
Alicja Maria Kuberska * Teresa E. Gallion * Joe Paire
Kimberly Burnham * Shareef Abdur – Rasheed
Ashok K. Bhargava * Elizabeth Castillo * Swapna Behera
Tezmin Ition Tsai * William S. Peters, Sr.

The Year of the Poet IX
December 2022

Featured Global Poets

Elarbi Abdelfattah * Lorraine Cragg
Neha Bhandarkar * Robert Gibbons

Climate Change Bees, Butterflies and Insect Life

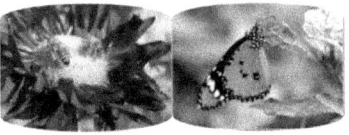

Poetry … Ekphrasticly Speaking

The Poetry Posse 2022

Gail Weston Shazor * Albert Carasco * Hülya N. Yılmaz
Jackie Davis Allen * Caroline Nazareno * Eliza Segiet
Alicja Maria Kuberska * Teresa E. Gallion * Joe Paire
Kimberly Burnham * Shareef Abdur – Rasheed
Ashok K. Bhargava * Elizabeth Castillo * Swapna Behera
Tezmin Ition Tsai * William S. Peters, Sr.

Now Available
www.innerchildpress.com/the-year-of-the-poet

Inner Child Press Anthologies

Now Available
www.innerchildpress.com/the-year-of-the-poet

Inner Child Press Anthologies

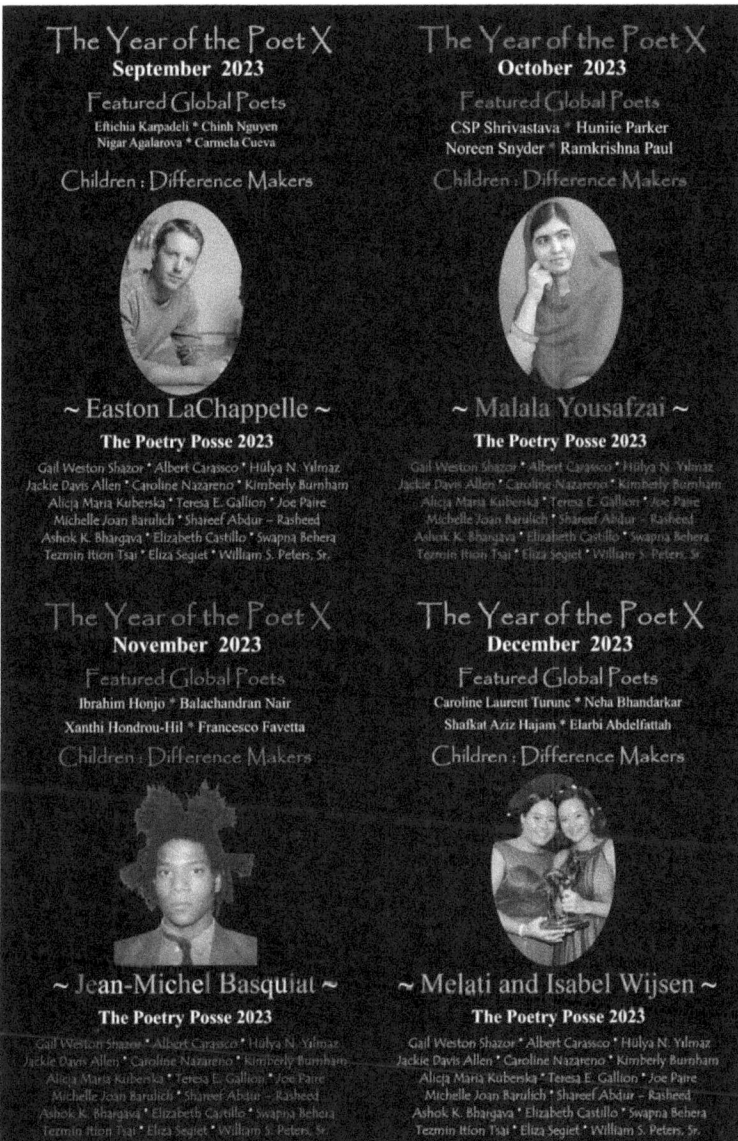

Now Available
www.innerchildpress.com/the-year-of-the-poet

Inner Child Press Anthologies

Now Available
www.innerchildpress.com/the-year-of-the-poet

Inner Child Press Anthologies

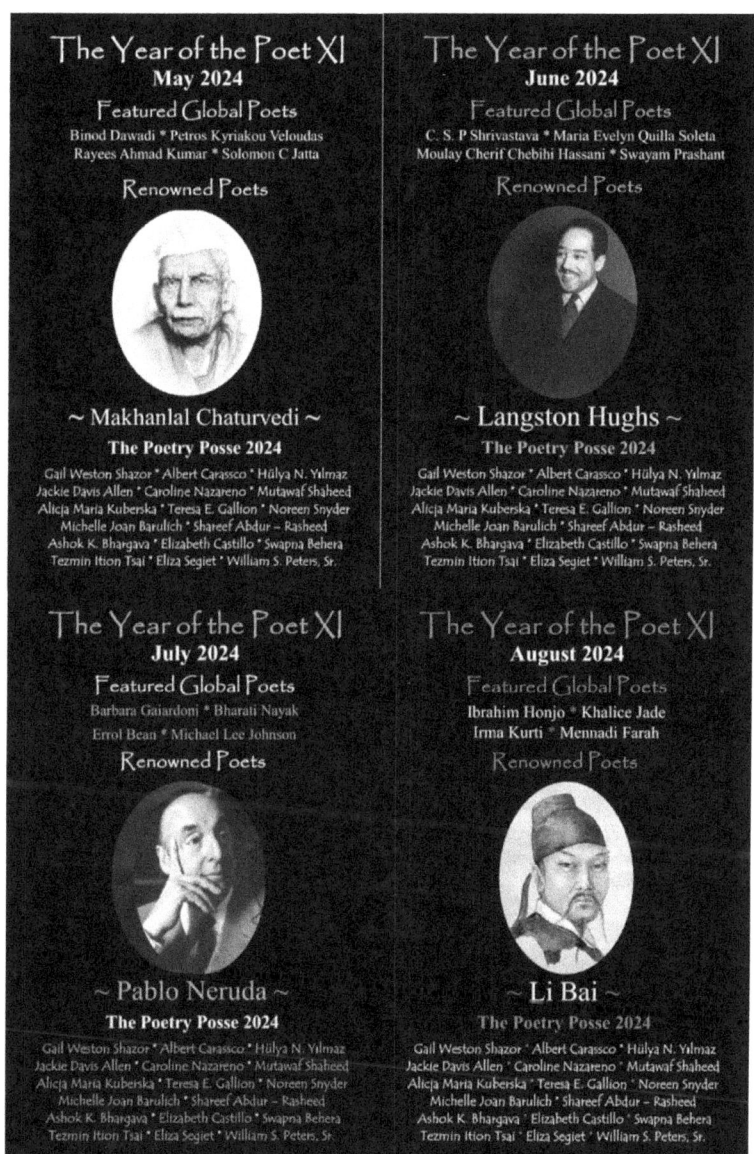

Now Available
www.innerchildpress.com/the-year-of-the-poet

Inner Child Press Anthologies

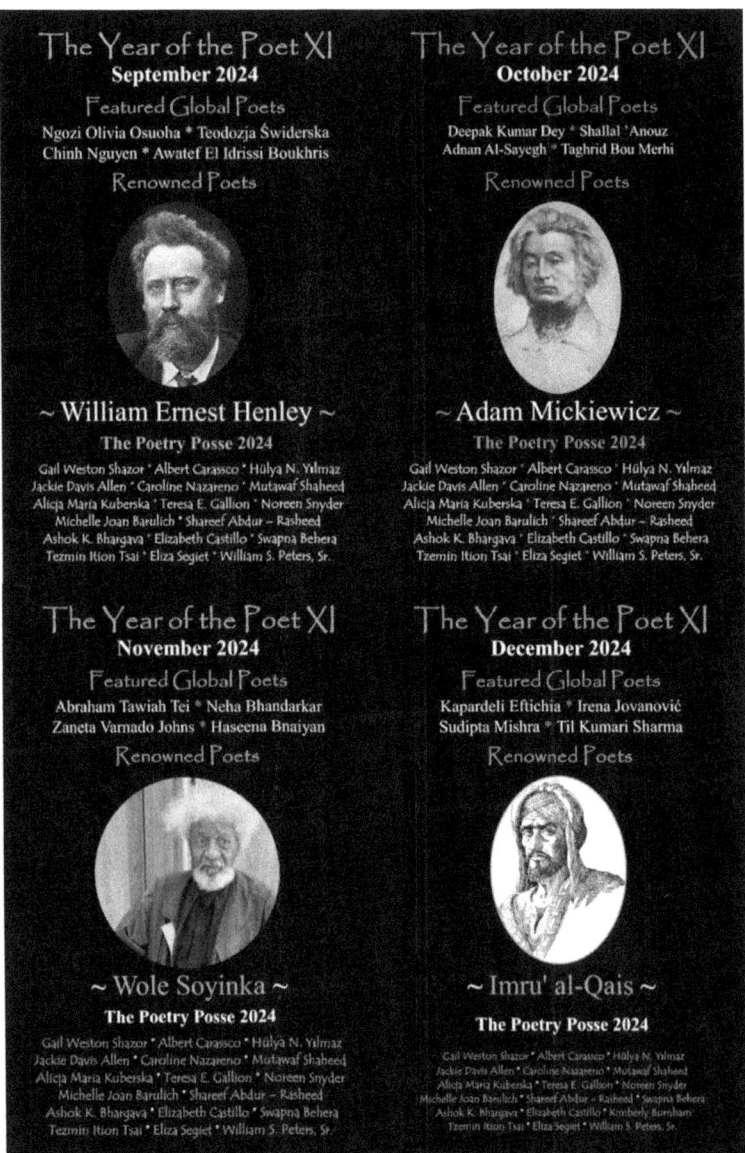

Now Available
www.innerchildpress.com/the-year-of-the-poet

and there is much, much more !

visit . . .

www.innerchildpress.com/anthologies-sales-special.php

Also check out our Authors and all the wonderful Books Available at :

www.innerchildpress.com/authors-pages

Inner Child Press Anthologies

Now Available

www.worldhealingworldpeacepoetry.com

Inner Child Press Anthologies

Now Available

www.worldhealingworldpeacepoetry.com

www.worldhealingworldpeacepoetry.com

World Healing World Peace
2012, 2014, 2016, 2018, 2020, 2022

Now Available

www.worldhealingworldpeacepoetry.com

Inner Child Press International

'building bridges of cultural understanding'

Meet the Board of Directors

William S. Peters, Sr.
Chair Person
Founder
Inner Child Enterprises
Inner Child Press

Hülya N Yılmaz
Director
Editing Services
Co-Chair Person

Fahredin B. Shehu
Director
Cultural Affairs

Elizabeth E. Castillo
Director
Recording Secretary

De'Andre Hawthorne
Director
Performance Poetry

Gail Weston Shazor
Director
Anthologies

Kimberly Burnham
Director
Cultural Ambassador
Pacific Northwest
USA

Ashok K. Bhargava
Director
WIN Awards

Deborah Smart
Director
Publicity
Marketing

www.innerchildpress.com

This Anthological Publication
is underwritten solely by

Inner Child Press International

Inner Child Press is a Publishing Company Founded and Operated by Writers. Our personal publishing experiences provides us an intimate understanding of the sometimes daunting challenges Writers, New and Seasoned may face in the Business of Publishing and Marketing their Creative "Written Work".

For more Information

Inner Child Press International

www.innerchildpress.com

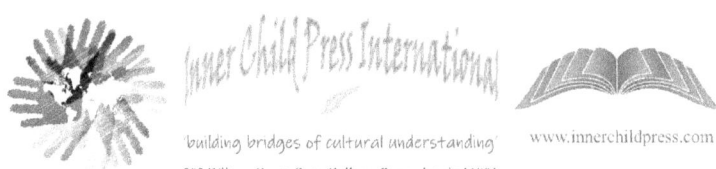

'building bridges of cultural understanding'
202 Wiltree Court, State College, Pennsylvania 16801

www.innerchildpress.com

~ fini ~